It is Written!

Spiritual Warfare Focusing on God and His Mighty Power!

by

Dr. James Lee

God has spoken, and Satan and his hosts of darkness have to be subject to His Word, "It is Written!"

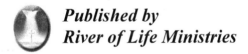

Published by
River of Life Ministries

Copyright © 2019 by Dr. James Lee

It is Written!
Spiritual Warfare Focusing on God and His Mighty Power
by Dr. James Lee

Printed in the United States of America

ISBN 978-1-7342549-0-7

All rights reserved solely by the author. The author guarantees all contents are original and do not infringe upon the legal rights of any other person or work. No part of this book may be reproduced in any form without the permission of the author. The views expressed in this book are not necessarily those of the publisher.

Unless otherwise indicated, Bible quotations are taken from The New King James Version of the Bible. Copyright © 1982 by Thomas Nelson Inc.

www.rlmva.org

ENDORSEMENTS

Dr. James Lee's new book "It is Written" explains the primary way Christians can resist the Devil's attempts to deceive and torment us: by using God's written words. This was the main defense strategy Jesus used when He was tempted by the Devil in the wilderness, as recorded in Matthew and Luke, chapter 4. For each temptation, Jesus quoted a verse from Deuteronomy and prefaced each verse with the Greek word *"grapho"*, which means "It is written." Jesus knew that the Devil could not defeat the power of God's written word. Dr. Lee wants us to know that, too. We all need to wield the authority of God's word to stand against the wiles of our common spiritual enemies. Dr. Lee knows all this not only from his biblical research but also from over 30 years of planting churches around the world while having victories over much spiritual warfare.

Dr. Lee also highlights the boundaries of our authority against spiritual forces of darkness. As most of us know, we have authority from Jesus "over unclean spirits, to cast them out" (Matt. 10:1). These are the demons that attack and infest human beings on a personal level. Jesus did not give us authority to cast out spiritual forces of darkness that have authority over regions and cities. Again, the written word of God is our guide. Nowhere in the Bible are God's people authorized to personally bind Satan or ruling spirits over regions and cast them out. When we personally attack those territorial spirits, we are operating outside of God's written, biblical boundaries for spiritual warfare. I have experienced the negative consequences of that unauthorized warfare myself. So, if you are interested in knowing the biblical foundation for the Christian's authority to defeat the schemes of the devil, "It is Written" will equip and protect you in the spiritual battles we all face in life."

Pastor Bob Fox
Abundant Life Fellowship
Chesapeake, VA

"It is Written" is an eye-opening, revelatory, refreshing book on the subject of spiritual warfare, deliverance, and effective praying. This book shows believers just what is our correct position in spiritual warfare. There has been such misconception about spiritual warfare and deliverance in the church. Dr. Lee's book refocuses our attention on the right person in charge—God! After 30 years of ministry in deliverance, I welcome this book because it teaches us how to stand in confidence, purpose, and authority when engaging in spiritual warfare. One of the high aspirations of this book is to reassure us how to pray in God's Divine ordinance.

I recommend this book to be in the curriculum in churches, Bible Schools, Mission programs, and Christian living. This book is a wonderful manual for Christian development. If you want to learn how to be an effective intercessor, work in the ministry of deliverance, a Christian interested in learning God's authority, or to understand more about the subject of spiritual warfare, please read this book. It will really change your perspective and life. Dr. James Lee's ministry in over 100 nations has prepared him to enhance his teaching with his exciting experiences in spiritual warfare.

This makes, "It is Written" one of the most valuable books in this season.

Dr. Brenda Stratton
President of Message to the Nations
Virginia Beach, VA

My husband and I have had the privilege of knowing Dr. Lee since 2008, and since then, we have had the further privilege of being mentored by him and his wife, Margarita. They truly have been nothing short of spiritual parents to us, for which we are forever grateful. Over the years, Dr. Lee has taught us many of the truths contained in this book, and I have learned so much about how to correctly and effectively engage in spiritual warfare from him. I am thrilled that Dr. Lee has memorialized his teachings on spiritual warfare in his book "It is Written", so that many others can experience the correct way to effectively engage in spiritual warfare and so that it can be studied and passed down through generations—including my own.

Kristen R. Jurjevich, Esq.
Virginia Beach, VA

There is a lot of confusion on spiritual warfare out there. Dr. Lee sets the record straight with this book. "It is Written" is very helpful in guiding one through spiritual battles and avoiding the dangerous pitfalls along the way. It focuses on leaning on God – after all, the battle belongs to the Lord. I have known Dr. Lee for over a decade and can attest that he is a man of God and that he practices what he teaches. I have seen him used by God in powerful ways domestically and abroad. His stories always fascinate and inspire me. He has been and is a blessing to my wife and me and has imparted valuable godly wisdom through the valleys and mountaintops in our journey of life. I hope this book will bless you as much as it has me.

Johan Jurjevich, MBA & CPA
Virginia Beach, VA

Dr. James Lee is a man of faith and integrity. I have known him for over thirty years and have had the privilege of ministering with him in Guatemala and India. His latest book, "It is Written," comes from the pages of Scriptures, his heart and his many years preaching, teaching and ministering in the nations. He writes about spiritual warfare from his personal encounters with the deceiver and the victory he has witnessed as people have been set free by the power of God from the works of the devil. "It is Written" is more than a story of his exploits; it is an instructional manual for you, the reader. For James desires that you, and all those to whom he is sent, become equipped with the Truth and empowers you to do spiritual warfare focusing on God and His mighty power.

The Rev. Dr. Jim Brown
Retired Executive Pastor of Church of the Messiah
Chesapeake, VA

Spiritual warfare is a key element of our true identity as disciples of Jesus Christ. We were created to be warriors! "It is Written" conveys the true nature of spiritual warfare. Dr. James Lee speaks with authority on this topic, not as an academic, but as one who has eaten the bread of life in the presence of his enemies. "It is Written" is a true treatise on spiritual warfare. You were created by God to continue Jesus' mission and destroy the works of the devil. Read "It is Written" to be equipped and encouraged on your mission.

Pete Matisoo
Captain (US Navy, Retired)
Virginia Beach, VA

"It is Written" is a biblically solid manuscript about spiritual warfare. If you remove the Scripture from this text, it would be less than half the size it is. Teaching such as this, which is so richly based in the Word of God, is needed in this hour. Hosea 4:6 says, *My people are destroyed for lack of knowledge...* I, like many others, have acted against the enemy beyond the limit of my authority to do so, and I paid a heavy price when I did!

So, I thank God for the wisdom and discernment found in these pages, so that others do not make the same foolish mistakes I did. I pray that you submit yourselves to this teaching in all humility so that you may be spared needless pain and suffering by following the ways of other foolish teachings on this subject. You can count on the words in this book to set you up for success. May the Bible verses contained in its pages give you the wisdom and knowledge for victory in the supernatural over the works of the devil and his evil forces, by the majesty and power found in the Name that is above every other name, the Lord Jesus Christ.

Rev. Jeffrey D. Crawford
Senior Leader, All Peoples Church
Lynchburg, VA

CONTENTS

Endorsements……………………………………………v

Introduction…………………………………………...xi

Chapter One……………………………………...17
God spoke and all things were created

Chapter Two……………………………………34
The battle belongs to the Lord

Chapter Three…………………………………...46
Satan has already been defeated

Chapter Four…………………………………...100
Dealing with Satan in the Old Testament

Chapter Five…………………………………...141
Dealing with Satan in the New Testament

INTRODUCTION

The history of mankind began with God's spoken word as written in Genesis 1:1, 3: *"In the beginning God created the heavens and the earth. Then God said, 'Let there be light' and there was light."* The whole Bible is written exactly according to what God said and declared by Himself or through His chosen priests, prophets, kings, apostles, and disciples. What the Father God, Jesus Christ and the Holy Spirit said was written by His chosen people as the Word of God and we can declare His words as "It is written!" The word of God transcends time, space and human understanding and what is written in the Bible must not be altered, modified, changed or rescinded by any other authority on the earth. God's word is the final answer. Satan, all of the hosts of evil power and wicked men cannot alter what God has established in the Bible for all of His creations in the heavens and the earth.

There have been too many books written about *"spiritual warfare against the devil and the power of darkness."* Those books have mostly focused (even magnified) the power of Satan more than the power of God. The Almighty God (Yahweh) created Lucifer as one of the archangels in heaven for His glory. When Lucifer fell from the glory of God, it was *El Shaddai* (the Almighty God) who cast him out of the kingdom of heaven into the earth. Ultimately, God will cast Satan, demons, false prophets and unbelievers into the lake of fire forever as stated in Revelation 20:10-15. Even though

Satan exercises his evil power over fallen mankind by enticing them with his deceptions, lies and manipulations, the Lord is in control over the history of mankind as the Alpha and the Omega, the Beginning and the End.

Some Christian leaders suggest that all the disasters, destructions, wars and injustices that have happened on the earth have been totally the work of the pure evil powers of the devil. If that were the case, then the Lord appears to not be directly in control or engaged in the affairs of the earth, and the devil is in absolute control over humanity to torment them as he wishes. The unfortunate result of the above notion can cause human beings to fear Satan more than the Creator God. I believe that Satan's evil power can be released against human beings when they are enticed by his wicked schemes and, thus, become his tools to carry out his evil plans on the earth. Regardless of what the devil does on the earth, the Bible states very clearly that the Lord is in charge over the affairs of mankind in Psalm 96:4-5, 9-10, 13:

> *For the Lord is great and greatly to be praised;* ***He is to be feared above all gods.*** *For all the gods of the peoples are idols but* ***the Lord made the heavens.*** *Oh, worship the Lord in the beauty of holiness! Tremble before Him, all the earth. Say among the nations,* ***"The Lord reigns; the world also is firmly established, it shall not be moved;*** *He shall judge the peoples righteously." For He is coming, for He is coming to judge the earth. He shall judge the world with righteousness, and the peoples with His truth.*

Therefore, if the Lord is in control over all the earth, then we must only fear Him and not the devil—the defeated enemy of God. However, by God's sovereign will, He has been allowing the devil and his demonic hosts to be engaged in the operation of human history until Revelation 20:10, *"And the devil, who deceived them, was cast into the lake of fire and brimstone where the beast and the false prophet are. And they will be tormented day and night forever and ever."*

Satan's main tool against humanity is "deception." Satan deceived Adam and Eve to disobey the commandment of God; consequently, the curse of death came down upon them and their descendants forever. Satan has always used his artful deception, lies and manipulation tactics to deceive as many human beings as he can in order to take them with him into the eternal lake of fire (Revelation 20:10). Eventually, Satan will be bound by an angel and cast into the bottomless pit in Revelation 20:1-3.

Can any believer in Christ bind Satan before his time? The answer is absolutely "No!" He cannot be bound until God will finally cast him into the lake of fire in the future. Until then, Satan will continuously exercise his evil power and influence over any man or woman who will surrender his or her will to follow the devil's wicked schemes instead of obeying the truth of the living God. Unfortunately, God will use Satan to separate His sheep from the goats. That means God will use Satan as His tool to bring about the final judgment upon fallen mankind—for those who follow the devil's deceptive ways will be cast into the lake of fire according to Revelation 20:11-15:

> *Then I saw a great white throne and Him who sat on it, from whose face the earth and the heaven fled away. And there was found no place for them. And I saw the dead, small and great, standing before God, and books were opened. And another book was opened, which is* **the Book of Life**. *And the dead were judged according to their works, by the things which were written in the books. The sea gave up the dead*

who were in it, and Death and Hades delivered up the dead who were in them. And they were judged, each one according to his works. Then Death and Hades were cast into the lake of fire. This is the second death. And **anyone not found written in the Book of Life was cast into the lake of fire.**

What is written in the Bible will take place whether you accept the truth or not. Because God is in control over the affairs of the whole of humanity, from the beginning in Genesis 1:1 to Revelation 22:21, we must fear the Lord and follow Him with all our hearts, minds and strength. No power on the earth can alter what God has written and established from the beginning. Whatever God does on the earth will always be led by His divine love as it is written in John 3:16, *"For God so loved the world that He gave His only begotten Son, that whoever believes in Him should not perish but have everlasting life."*

Also, God is patiently waiting for the gospel of the kingdom to be preached in all the world as a witness to all the **nations** (in Greek *ethne*: every people group) according to Matthew 24:14, then the end will come (that means Jesus Christ will come back once that happens). Therefore, the Scripture declares God's loving heart for the fallen mankind in 2 Peter 3:9, *"The Lord is not slack concerning His promise, as some count slackness, but is long-suffering toward us, not willing that any should perish but that all should come to repentance."*

God loves all of His created peoples, tongues, tribes and nations. However, God's divine love for all of the fallen mankind can only be realized if they repent of their sins, turn away from their wicked ways, come to the cross of Christ to receive the forgiveness of their sins, and accept His redeeming grace of eternal life in Christ. Only then will they appropriate God's divine love for their lives in order to receive abundant life on the earth and eternal life in heaven. But if one only claims "God is love" for one's life without turning away from one's wicked ways, then John 3:18 will be fulfilled in one's life, *"but he who does not believe is condemned already, because he has not believed in the name of the only begotten Son of God."*

The consequence of anyone who doesn't accept Jesus Christ as his or her Lord and Savior will result in him or her rejecting God's divine provision of salvation (His ultimate love). If he or she lives as a god of his or her own life, then the ultimate fruit of that lifestyle will eventually lead him or her to eternal damnation in the lake of fire. Therefore, God has given His disciples the Great Commission in Matthew 28:18-20 and Acts 1:8. God has imparted His kingdom authority and power to His disciples in order for them to expand His kingdom to the ends of the earth with signs, wonders, and miracles following.

That means the followers of Jesus Christ must do everything they can to preach the Gospel of the kingdom of God to every unreached people group in the world by destroying the works of the devil in accordance with Matthew 10:7-8, *"And as you go, preach, saying, 'The kingdom of heaven is at hand.' Heal the sick, cleanse the lepers, raise the dead, cast out demons. Freely you have received, freely give."*

Therefore, believers in Christ must focus on God's divine authority and power to destroy the works of the devil by evangelizing the world. When we are engaging in all sorts of spiritual battles in life, we must focus on becoming strong in the Lord and in the power of His might (Ephesians 6:10), and not focus on Satan and his evil hosts of darkness. In this book, I will use the Scriptures as the most important references to magnify the Lord, as I describe how the heroes of the Bible conducted their spiritual warfare so we can learn from their examples how to apply their principles to our spiritual struggles in life.

"***The battle belongs to the Lord!*** (1 Samuel 17:47)"

Chapter 1

GOD SPOKE AND ALL THINGS WERE CREATED

God is the Author over the affairs of all created beings and things in the heavens and the earth. The triune God (the Father, Jesus Christ the Son and the Holy Spirit) has the ultimate authority and power over the activities in the heavenly and earthly realms. From the beginning of creation, God spoke and all things were established according to His divine power. What was written in the Bible reveals God's divine vision, mission and action plans for His created beings. God's written words will be fulfilled in His divine time for His glory and no powers in the heavens or on the earth can alter His supreme will and purposes.

Therefore, Matthew 24:35 states, *"I tell you the truth, until heaven and earth disappear, not even the smallest detail of God's law will disappear until its purpose is achieved. (NLT)"* The visible and invisible world has been created by the triune God according to the creation account in Genesis 1:1-3, *"In the beginning God created the heavens and the earth. The earth was without form, and void; and darkness was on the face of the deep. And the Spirit of God was hovering over the face of the waters. Then God said, 'Let there be light'; and there was light."* What we see in the visible world had been created by God's spoken words. As we examine the creation stories in the Bible, we can also comprehend that, the Holy Spirit and Jesus Christ, the Son, were also actively engaged in the process of the creation with the Father God:

> Psalm 104:30, *"You send forth **Your Spirit**, they are created; and You renew the face of the earth."*

> Isaiah 40:18, 22, 26, *"To whom then will you liken God? Or what likeness will you compare to Him? It is He who sits above the circle of the earth, and its inhabitants are like grasshoppers, who stretches out the heavens like a curtain, and spreads them out like a tent to dwell in. Lift up your eyes on high and see who has created these things, who brings out their host by number; He calls them all by name, by the greatness of His might and the strength of His power; not one is missing."*

> Colossians 1:15-17, *"He (Jesus Christ) is the image of the invisible God, the firstborn over all creation. For **by Him all things were created** that are in heaven and that are on earth, visible and invisible, whether thrones or dominions or principalities or powers. **All things were created through Him and for Him**. And He is before all things, and in Him all things consist."*

Now, let's discover together how awesome and mighty God, who controls all the movements and affairs of the universe, is! Jesus Christ states in Matthew 11:25, *"I thank You, Father, Lord of heaven and earth..."* The Psalmist declared in Psalm 102:19, *"For He looked down from the height of His sanctuary; from heaven the Lord viewed the earth."* Also, King David proclaimed in Psalm 103:19, *"The

Lord has established His throne in heaven, and His kingdom rules over all." In the book of Daniel 4:34-35, the Gentile king Nebuchadnezzar praises Yahweh, the God of Israel, as the One and only Creator God: *"For **His dominion is an everlasting dominion and His kingdom is from generation to generation**. All the inhabitants of the earth are reputed as nothing; He does according to His will in the army of heaven and among the inhabitants of the earth. No one can restrain His hand or say to Him, 'What have You done?'"*

According to the word of God in Hebrews 11:3, we can also understand that the entire universe was formed at God's command. That means God controls the total affairs and movements of the whole universe:

> *By faith we understand that the entire universe was formed at God's command, that what we now see did not come from anything that can be seen.*

POWER OF GOD CONTROLS THE UNIVERSE

Astronomers, using the Hubble Space Telescope to examine the observable universe in 2013, stated that there are over 225 billion galaxies in the universe. They also discovered that there are over 200 billion stars and over 100 billion Solar Systems in a Milky Way Galaxy alone. However, the boundary of the universe that we can see through the Hubble Space Telescope is limited by how far it is capable of viewing within the observable universe.

That means the entire universe may be thousands of times bigger and wider than what we can observe at this present time. Regardless of its size, God is absolutely in control over the whole universe. He is the omnipotent (all-powerful and almighty), omnipresent (ubiquitous, infinite and boundless) and omniscient (all-knowing and all-seeing) God. There is no limit to God. He can travel through the whole universe to come to the earth in a split second. How marvelous and great is our mighty God! Well, let me elaborate God's greatness a little bit further. Do you know how far it is to the edge of the Solar System from the earth?

The website "livescience.com" declares, *"At this very moment, Voyager 1 and 2, two space crafts that left Earth in the 1977, are exiting the solar system. They are passing through the magnetic bubbles at its edge approximately nine billion miles from Earth."* That means these spacecrafts have been traveling for over 40 years to reach the edge of our Solar System. Can you imagine how long it will take at this speed if they try to reach the heaven where God dwells? But to our total amazement, our prayers can reach the throne room of God instantly and His angels can come from heaven to assist His chosen people just as quickly.

Do you know that the earth rotates in about 24 hours at a speed of just over 1,000 miles per hour? Not only that, the earth is also moving around the sun at about 67,000 miles per hour right now. Wow! Can you feel the movement of the earth under your feet now? Who controls the locations, movements, the perfect gravity pulls, and distances among the sun, moon and earth? I believe it is the power of the Holy Spirit that controls so that they are in perfect positions with the absolute balance of gravity pulls and movements in the midst of space so that none of them ever collide with each other.

Obviously, the Creator God rules over the heavens and the earth. In 2016, when astronomers gathered the data from the NASA's Hubble Space Telescope and other observatories, they came to the surprising conclusion that there are at least two trillion galaxies in the universe (excerpt from www.nasa.gov). It expanded 10 times greater than the 2013 reports. In the next 20 years, as more powerful telescopes than Hubble may be developed, the span of the universe may potentially expand 100 times greater than now. God is in absolute control over the universe with His mighty power as Psalm 103:19 describes, *"The Lord has made the heavens His throne; from there He rules over everything.* (NLT)" Therefore, a created being such as the devil is no match to the Creator God.

THE NAMES OF THE CREATOR GOD

Throughout the Old Testament, various names of God were written for His chosen people so they could have total confidence in the powerful meanings behind His names. God's diverse names represent His attributes such as divine authority, power, righteousness, holiness, peace, grace, mercy, love, etc. Therefore, as children of God, we must understand His divine names so we can live a victorious Christian life according to His provisions in His powerful names. Let's examine some of the names of the almighty God:

- **YAHWEH** – I AM WHO I AM, the personal name of God (Exodus 3:14-15): If we put our total confidence in the GREAT I AM, then whatever we need, we can apply His name in all our situations to receive His blessings: if you need salvation, then God is to you as "I AM your salvation." If you need deliverance from the power of darkness, then God is to you as "I AM your deliverer" and He will rescue you from the trap of the devil. If you need healing, then God is to you as "I AM your healer."

Whatever circumstance that you may be under, if you repent of your sinful lifestyle and turn to Him with all your heart and mind, then you can have the GREAT I AM to be what you need Him to be as your Creator, Savior, Deliverer, Provider, Healer, Protector, Banner, Sanctifier, Shepherd, etc.

- **ELOHIM** – The Creator God (a plural noun: triune God), mighty and strong (Genesis 1:1; 17:7): Genesis 1:1-2, *"In the beginning God* (ELOHIM: the triune God – the Father, Jesus Christ and the Holy Spirit) *created the heavens and the earth. The earth was without form, and void; and darkness was on the face of the deep. And the Spirit of God was hovering over the face of the waters."* The Father and the Holy Spirit were clearly engaged in the creation according to Genesis 1:1-2.

    Additionally, according to the Scripture in Colossians 1:16, Jesus Christ was also in the creation with Father and the Holy Spirit, *"For by Him* (Jesus Christ) *all things were created that are in heaven and that are on earth, visible and invisible, whether thrones or dominions or principalities or powers. All things were created through Him and for Him."* Therefore, if we put our total faith in the CREATOR, we do not need to fear anything in this world because He is in absolute control over the affairs of the universe including the earth and your life.

- **EL SHADDAI** – God Almighty (Genesis 49:24): *"By the hands of the Mighty* (EL SHADDAI) *God of Jacob."* The Hebrew word *"abir"* has a meaning of God protecting Jacob under His wings (feathers); thus, it can be translated as "Mighty God who protects" or "Mighty God the Protector" according to *"Abarim Publication*—Biblical Name Vault: Abir." During my over 30 years of missions work in the nations, El Shaddai has supernaturally protected me from many wicked evil schemes of the devil. When I was ministering in Kathmandu, Nepal, in September 2004, Maoist guerrillas surrounded the capital city of Kathmandu and threatened to blow up any cars driving in the city. After the threat, the whole city was paralyzed with fear and no car was driving through the city. I was there with my wife and four other American friends to conduct a one-week leadership conference for over 100 pastors and leaders in Kathmandu. I hired a Christian Taxi driver who would risk his own life to drive us to the conference place, where all the participants were staying at around 8:00 a.m. and then bring us back to the hotel at around 5:30 p.m. each day.

Each night we walked to a local Internet café to check our emails and to respond to the senders. It was on Wednesday night after dinner when we were going to walk to the Internet café. As we were about to leave the hotel gate, the Holy Spirit spoke to me very clearly that we were to walk to the café not by the usual route (right turn from the gate) that would take less than 10 minutes to walk, but rather we were to take the long way around (the left turn) to get there which would take approximately 30 minutes. I felt the urgency from the Holy Spirit to obey His still small voice so I told the rest of the team that we had to walk to the café the long way around that night. They complained to me about why they had to go around the long way to get there. Reluctantly, they followed me to the left turn from the hotel gate to the long way to get there.

After we had walked on for about 5 minutes, we heard a very loud explosion. We didn't know where it was coming from. The next morning, as we were having breakfast at the hotel restaurant, we saw a picture of a car in which a bomb had exploded on the front cover of an English newspaper. The paper described that the explosion took place between our hotel and the Internet café at the same time we had been walking to the place. If we would have gone to the café by our usual route (right turn from the hotel gate), we would have been the victims of the car bomb explosion. El Shaddai divinely protected us from the imminent danger of the explosion as our God Almighty that night. No wicked schemes of the devil will prevail against you if El Shaddai goes with you wherever you go and protects you with His mighty power.

- **YAHWEH-JIREH** – The Lord will Provide (Genesis 22:14): After God substituted a ram for Isaac as a burnt offering in Genesis 22:12-13, Abraham called the name of the place as "The-Lord-Will-Provide." No matter what circumstances we may be in, if we put our total faith in YAHWEH-JIREH, He will supernaturally provide all our needs according to His riches in glory (Philippians 4:19).

  When I came to study at Regent University in March 1987, I had a very difficult time finding a part-time job to support my family for three months. I was very frustrated with God and myself so I cried out to Him one day, *"Why are You not helping me to find any job to pay for my tuition and to support my family?"* God told me that He had to train me to totally depend on Him for all my financial needs while I was going through my Master's degree in World Missions. He did this so that when He called me to carry out His missions to the nations after the graduation, I would know how to totally depend on Him to take care of the entire ministry needs as well as my family's. Therefore, God told me not to work at all while I was studying for my degree at Regent University because He was my Yahweh-Jireh.

It was at first very difficult to understand God's ways for dealing with His provisions. By His supernatural grace, I finished my Master's degree in one and a half years without working at all. Surely, He did provide for all our needs according to riches in His glory during those days. Whenever we had any needs, we simply prayed for God to provide according to His perfect ways. Then my Christian friends would send checks in my name stating that they were led by the Holy Spirit to send them for whatever we needed at that time. Because of what I had to learn to totally depend on Him for my family's daily needs while I was attending Regent University, I have been able to carry out His missions to the nations in faith for the past 31 years—truly Yahweh-Jireh provides.

- **YAHWEH-RAPHA** – The Lord who heals (Exodus 15:26): *"If you diligently heed the voice of the Lord your God and do what is right in His sight, give ear to His commandments and keep all His statutes, I will put none of the diseases on you which I have brought on the Egyptians. For **I am the Lord who heals you**."* It is God's absolute desire to give His children divine health as well as healing when they become sick. However, God has conditional prerequisite clauses in order for them to receive His divine health and healing—diligently heed the voice of the Lord your God, do what is right in His sight, give ear to His commandments, and keep all His statutes.

As I have traveled to over 100 countries in the world, I have witnessed Yahweh-Rapha moving in His divine power to open blind eyes, deaf ears, heal crippled legs, and cast out many demons in the mission fields. One of the most incredible encounters with Yahweh-Rapha took place when I was driving through a remote Mayan village in Guatemala in February 1991. I was with my wife,

Margarita and an American missionary (I will call him "Mike"). As we were driving through a Quiche tribe Mayan village, Mike stopped the car in front of a local Quiche clinic and suggested we go in and check it out. My whole body was covered with dust and I was so sweaty that I told Mike I did not want to go in there. However, he insisted for Margarita and I to go in and see the condition of the poor clinic.

We reluctantly went into the clinic which was very muggy and filthy without any air conditioning. A very pungent smell caused us to be nauseous as we entered. A nurse came to me and asked if I was a minister. I was very surprised that she could recognize me as a minister when I was agitated by the very poor condition of the clinic. She asked me to pray for a dying 16-year-old girl in a bed. I only wanted to get out of that filthy clinic as quickly as possible when she asked me. I had no faith to pray for her healing. The nurse literally dragged me to her bedside. Margarita and I felt God's compassionate heart coming over us for her. We led her to the Lord first and prayed for her to be healed in a very faithless and ritualistic way. After the prayer, we got up and quickly began to walk toward the exit door. All of a sudden, we heard commotions behind us so we turned around to see what was going on. To our great surprise, the young lady got up out of her bed and she told the nurse that she was totally healed.

At the same time, Mike brought a 10-year-old boy who was paralyzed in a wheel chair. We prayed for him and he got up out of the chair and began to run around the clinic. I repented of my bad attitude of not wanting to pray for the young lady because I didn't feel any faith in me. After that experience, I realized that healing comes from the Lord—Yahweh-Rapha. Regardless of my bad attitude and lack of faith, God loved the young girl and boy so much that He wanted to bring His divine healing for them through us. All God needed was for any available vessels to be His agents to manifest His glory.

- **YAHWEH-NISSI** – The Lord Our Banner (Exodus 17:15): After the Lord assured Moses that he would utterly blot out the remembrance of Amalek from under heaven in Exodus 17:14, Moses built an altar and called its name, THE-LORD-IS-MY-BANNER (vs. 15). If the Lord is your Banner and He fights the battle for you, then no weapon formed against you shall prosper (Isaiah 54:17). During the battles that Moses and the Israelites encountered in their journey through the wilderness, the pillar of fire by night and the pillar of smoke by day, Yahweh-Nissi went with them and fought their battles for them. Therefore, no kingdoms around them could defeat them because Yahweh-Nissi was with them. As you walk with Yahweh-Nissi throughout the journey of your life, He will go before you and fight the spiritual battles for you for His glory. We only need to trust God in all our ways and move very carefully with Him every step in our journey of life.

- **YAHWEH-M'KADDESH** – The Lord who Sanctifies (Leviticus 20:8): The Lord said to the Israelites in Leviticus 20:7-8, *"Consecrate yourselves therefore, and be holy, for I am the Lord your God. And you shall keep My statutes, and perform them:* ***I am the Lord who sanctifies you.***" As the Holy God indwells inside of His children, it is He who makes them holy and sanctifies them for His glory. We cannot make ourselves holy and pure before God with our own righteousness and will power. Only He who lives inside of us is holy and His holiness sanctifies us as we separate ourselves totally unto Him. Let Yahweh-M'Kaddesh shine His holiness through you and sanctify you as His vessel of honor for His glory so you can shine His light before men wherever you may go.

- **YAHWEH-SHALOM** – The Lord Our Peace (Judges 6:24): After Gideon saw the Angel of the Lord, he was afraid that he might die in Judges 6:23-24, so God said to him, *"Peace be with you; do not fear, you shall not die." So Gideon built an altar there to the Lord, and called it* **The-Lord-Is-Peace**.*"* If the Lord chooses to use you for His glory and you are blameless before Him, then you have no need to be afraid because He comes to you as "The Lord is Peace." Also Jesus Christ, the Prince of Peace, promised in John 14:27, *"Peace I leave with you, My peace I give to you; not as the world gives do I give to you. Let not your heart be troubled, neither let it be afraid."*

  After Jesus Christ was resurrected and first reappeared to His disciples, He said, *"Peace be with you."* According to Strong's Concordance 7965, *Shalom* means completeness, wholeness, health, peace, welfare, safety, soundness, tranquility, prosperity, perfectness, fullness, harmony, rest, and the absence of agitation or discord. *Shalom* comes from the root verb *shalam* meaning to be complete, to make whole, perfect and full. Therefore, when Yahweh-Shalom comes into your life, you can enjoy all of the above blessings of *Shalom*.

- **YAHWEH-TSIDKENU** – The Lord Our Righteousness (Jeremiah 33:15-16): *"In those days and at that time I will cause to grow up to David a Branch of righteousness; He (Jesus Christ) shall execute judgment and righteousness* *in the earth. In those days Judah will be saved, and Jerusalem will dwell safely. And this is the name by which she will be called: THE LORD OUR RIGHTEOUSNESS.*" As the Lord Jesus Christ indwells believers, "the Lord Our Righteousness" takes our sins away by His own blood and provides His righteousness to reign in our lives so we can live for His glory and expand His kingdom on earth.

When I was growing up in a Buddhist home in Seoul, South Korea, I tried to understand Buddhism and its core belief system. When I found out that I had to do everything possible to get rid of all of my desires to be free from the curses of the cycle of life, I quickly found out that it was impossible for me to do that with my own willpower. No matter how hard I tried to deliver myself from all my evil desires, I quickly fell into an even more sinful lifestyle.

After I came to America, I was introduced to Christianity for the first time in a very real way. As I read the New Testament for the first time, I began to discover that Jesus Christ died for my sins on the cross and all I needed to do was to repent of all my sins and to accept Him as my Lord and Savior. Then, He would forgive me of all my sins and cleanse me from all my unrighteousness. And when the power of the Holy Spirit came down upon me, it was God the Holy Spirit who empowered me to overcome my evil desires. Once I understood God's grace was available for such a sinner like me, I surrendered my life to the Lord—Yahweh-Tsidkenu became my righteousness to live for His glory since January 1977.

- **YAHWEH-ROHI** – The Lord Our Shepherd (Psalm 23:1-2): *"The Lord is my Shepherd; I shall not want. He*

makes me to lie down in green pastures; He leads me beside the still waters." If the Lord is your Shepherd, you do not need to be worried or afraid because He will guide you through green pastures in which you will be well taken care of all the days of your life. And He will also lead you to the still waters where you can always have more than enough water to drink from the "Fountain of Living Water." Thus, you will say, *"Surely goodness and mercy shall follow me all the days of my life; and I will dwell in the house of the Lord forever* (Psalm 23:6)."
For the past 42 years in Christ, Yahweh-Rohi has truly guided my life through His divine green pastures as my Shepherd.

- **YAHWEH-SABAOTH** – The Lord of the Hosts (Isaiah 1:24): *"Therefore the Lord says, the Lord of hosts, the Mighty One of Israel, 'Ah, I will rid Myself of My adversaries, and take vengeance on My enemies."* When enemies rose up against the Israelites during the Old Testament days, the Lord mustered the armies of the heaven, on several occasions, to destroy their wicked plans against His chosen people. Truly if God is for you, who can be against you (Romans 8:31)?" If the Lord fights the battle for you, then you can truly say, *"No weapon formed against me shall prosper, and every tongue which rises against me in judgment the Lord shall condemn* (Isaiah 54:17)."

  During the past 31 years of my missions work in the nations, God has sent His angels to protect me on several occasions. One time I was ministering in a Muslim village in Ethiopia and I had a chance to lead a young Muslim lady to the Lord. The following night, while I was having an altar call for Ethiopians to surrender their lives to the Lord, many of them ran to the altar to accept Jesus Christ as their Lord and Savior. Suddenly, one man came out of the crowd and ran toward me. When he came within a foot of me, a big machete fell out of his jacket and landed on the ground. At first his eyes were filled with anger toward me and he stared at me as though he was going to kill me. However, within a couple of minutes, his whole demeanor changed and he, too, surrendered his life to the Lord with tears flowing down his face.

After dinner the pastor of the church told me that the man with the machete was the father of the converted Muslim girl. He told the pastor that he came to kill me that night but when he came near me, an invisible power knocked his machete to the ground and at that moment he saw two giant angels with flaming swords drawn in their hands behind me. And he heard a voice telling him that he needed to surrender his life to the Lord Jesus Christ. When I heard that, chills ran down my spine and I began to praise the Lord (Yahweh-Sabaoth) for sending His angels to protect me that night!

GOD RULES OVER THE KINGDOMS OF MEN

God also rules in the kingdom of men according to Daniel 4:17b, *"In order that the living may know that the Most High rules in the kingdom of men, gives it to whomever He will, and sets over it the lowest of men."* That means God is also in absolute control over the affairs of the kingdoms of men. We may not be able to fully understand why God would set up such wicked kings and kingdoms in this world. However, when we get to heaven, I believe, our eyes will be opened and we will understand the full wisdom of God over matters that we can hardly comprehend in this world. Nevertheless, every living human being will know that the Most High God rules over the kingdoms of men and it is He who gives earthly kingdoms to whomever He choose for His glory. Not only that, God's dominion over the kingdoms of men is an everlasting dominion according to Daniel 4:34b-35:

> *For His dominion is an everlasting dominion, and His kingdom is from generation to generation. All the inhabitants of the earth are reputed as nothing;* **He does according to His will in the army of heaven and among the inhabitants of the earth**. *No one can restrain His hand or say to Him, "What have You done?*

It is obvious that God is the Creator of the universe and He has the authority, right and power to do whatever He chooses with His created kingdoms, peoples, tongues, tribes and nations. No one can say to the Creator, *"What have You done or Why have you done this or that?"* He is the Creator and we are simply His created human beings. We need to humble ourselves and obey His ways, laws, statutes, and commandments for His good pleasure and glory.

In any battle the greater power wins. The main emphasis of this book is on the power of God that is infinitely greater than any power that can come against Him. The secondary emphasis is on the delegated authority and power God has made available to His sons and daughters to make them "more than conquerors" over all spiritual foes (Romans 8:37) as they carefully obey His commandments. Every war involves two opposing powers; only one side can win. In spiritual war, we see the power of God and His army pitted against the power of the devil and his army. God's army is comprised of the holy angels and the Saints of God; Satan's army is comprised of his evil angels and all unbelievers.

Some who do not know God have posited a dualism that portrays the devil as the equal of God. Satan is in no way a match for God! Satan is a created being, created by God and controlled by God. As a fallen angel, Satan retains only as much of his original angelic power as God has allowed. He can do nothing to a Saint except as God permits. The Bible is our spiritual military manual. The Word of God guarantees victory to those who obey its instructions.

The history of Israel is the story of warfare, victories, and some defeats. God told them to go in and possess the Promised Land. As long as they were obedient, no power could stop them. God has not told us to possess a physical land; He has told us to "***go into all the world and preach the gospel to every creature***" (Mark 16:15). As we obey God's commandments and do according to His instructions, we can be victorious over the powers of darkness throughout the journey of our lives. However, if we do not carefully follow the commandments written in our spiritual military manual (the Bible), then we can suffer loss in our spiritual warfare.[1]

Chapter 2

THE BATTLE BELONGS TO THE LORD

The horse is prepared for the day of battle, but deliverance is of the Lord (Proverb 21:31). During the journey of this short life on the earth, the children of God will go through numerous spiritual battles thrown at them by the power of darkness. Therefore, we need to put on the whole armor of God so that we are able to stand firm against the evil forces of darkness by totally depending on God's wisdom, power, authority and protection to defeat them. We need to be spiritually prepared to face the battle each day, but we also must know for sure that our victory and deliverance comes from the Lord.

If we put our total trust in the Lord and pray according to His perfect will by absolutely relying on His power and authority against the devil, then He will fight the battle for us so that He can receive all the glory. For example, God fought the battle for the Israelites when they were chased by the Egyptians in front of the Red Sea in Exodus 14:13-14, *"And Moses said to the people, 'Do not be afraid. Stand still, and see the salvation of the Lord, which He will accomplish for you today.* **The Lord will fight for you, and you shall hold your peace.**" However, the devil wants to draw God's elect away from totally relying on God during spiritual warfare. Rather Satan's desire is for them to fight directly against him or his principalities, powers, rulers of the darkness of this age, or spiritual hosts of wickedness in the heavenly places. If we initiate an unauthorized fight directly against the devil and his hosts of wickedness (in the second heavenly realm) without depending on the Lord to fight the battle for us, then they can overpower us and cause us to be severely afflicted by them. The result of engaging in an unauthorized battle directly against the devil can cause us to fall from the glory of God—His presence will not go with us.

The late John Paul Jackson said, *"Who are you to taunt Satan? Who are you to imagine that you can capture Satan or tame him as if he were an animal or kill him by throwing harpoons at him?"* To attempt such things is being full of presumption, vain imagination and false hope" as Job 41:1-2, 7, 9-11 describes about Leviathan which is a metaphor for Satan[2]:

> *Can you draw out Leviathan with a hook, or snare his tongue with a line which you lower? Can you put a reed through his nose, or pierce his jaw with a hook? Can you fill his skin with harpoons, or his head with fishing spears? Lay your hand on him; remember the battle—never do it again! Indeed, any hope of overcoming him is vain; Shall one not be overwhelmed at the sight of him? No one is so fierce that he would dare stir him up. Who then is able to stand against Me? Who has preceded Me, that I should pay him? Everything under heaven is Mine.*

Numerous books have been written about the subject of "Spiritual Warfare." However, many of these books teach Christian intercessors to rise up and fight directly against

Satan, principalities, powers and spiritual hosts of darkness in the heavenly places. Some of these books instruct us to bind Satan and principalities over a city, region or even a nation in the name of Jesus Christ. The hypothesis behind these popular spiritual warfare doctrines is based on the fact that believers have the authority and power of Jesus Christ on earth so we can bind Satan, principalities and powers of the air in His name. In so doing, more often than not, these books magnify the direct spiritual warfare against the devil and his evil power of darkness instead of glorifying the Lord and His indestructible kingdom authority and power in heaven and on earth. Also, it entices spiritual warfare intercessors to become proud and to demonstrate their unbiblical authority against the devil to draw attention to themselves.

BELIEVERS IN CHRIST ONLY HAVE GOD'S DELEGATED AUTHORITY AND POWER

We must understand that Jesus Christ has all authority in heaven and on earth according to Matthew 28:18 and the Holy Spirit has all power in heaven and on earth. Of course, Jesus Christ lives inside of us with His full authority and the Holy Spirit indwells us with His full power. However, followers of Christ do not have all authority and power over Satan on earth. If we were to have all authority and power in heaven and on earth, then we would be gods and not men.

Believers in Christ can only have the delegated authority of Christ and power of the Holy Spirit on earth. We can only exercise the authority of Christ and the power of the Holy Spirit as God imparts them to us to destroy the works of the devil in the name of Jesus Christ and according to the written words of God in the Bible. We cannot engage in a spiritual battle that has not been authorized by the Lord and word of God. Jesus Christ said in John 12:49, *"For I have not spoken on My own authority; but the Father who sent Me gave Me a command, what I should say and what I should speak."* Also, Jesus said in John 5:19, *"Most assuredly, I say to you, **the Son can do nothing of himself;** but what he sees the Father do; for whatever He does, the Son also does in like manner."* If the Son of the living God could not do anything on His own authority but only what He saw His Father doing, then how much more should we only do what we see Jesus doing through the guidance of the Holy Spirit.

There is not a Scripture in the whole Bible that directly instructs the followers of Christ to bind Satan or principalities or the rulers of darkness of this age. If there was anyone who could bind Satan it was Jesus Christ. Before Jesus Christ went to the cross, He rebuked Satan by simply saying, *"It is written"* in Matthew 4:4, 7 and 10. After the devil left Jesus Christ, angels came and ministered to Him (Matthew 4:11).

In the Gospel accounts, we see Jesus Christ confronting the kingdom of darkness everywhere He went. Jesus came not only to proclaim the Kingdom of God, but to demonstrate it and to establish it on the earth. The battle went from a totally defensive strategy to one of offense. Confronting the works of the devil and destroying them, Jesus healed the sick, raised the dead, and cast out demons. These were the signs of the Kingdom, all of which had been prophesied. Not only did Jesus do these things, He taught and commissioned His disciples to do the same things.

However, the outcome of any spiritual warfare rests on how a man would yield his will to God or Satan. Prior to the fall of man, the will of man was to be the expression of the will of God. If Satan were going to get his will done on earth, he would have to get it done through the will of man. God, having turned dominion power over every living thing on the earth to man (Genesis 1:28), also had to work through man to get His will done on earth. The battle between God and Satan comes down to the battle over the will of man. The prize of the battle is the will of man. God is looking for a man who will do His will. Satan is looking for a man who will do his will.[3]

Therefore, when God finds a man who will obey His every command and willfully chooses to do His will, then He will release His delegated authority and power to destroy the works of the devil on the earth to expand the Kingdom of God to the ends of the earth. If we want to see God moving in His divine authority and power in our lives, then we have to be humble, obedient, loyal and committed servants of God doing exactly what He authorizes us to do.

THE HEAVENLY REALM BELONGS TO THE LORD

Believers in Christ received the authority to expand the kingdom of heaven on the earth by preaching the gospel of the kingdom and by destroying the works of the devil. Psalm 115:16 confirms that God has given the earth to His children, **"The heaven, even the heavens, are the Lord's; but the earth He has given to the children of men."** However, God never gave His children authority or power over the forces in heavenly places. The heavens belong to the Lord. Therefore, warfare in the second heaven realm also belongs to Him.

Demons are referred to as "unclean spirits" in Matthew 10:1; Mark 1:27; 3:11; 5:13; Acts 5:16; "wicked or evil spirit" in Luke 7:21; 8:2; Acts 19:12-13; "spirit of divination in Acts 16:16; "deceiving spirits" in 1 Timothy 4:1; "the spirit of error" in 1 John 4:6; and "spirits of demons" in Revelation

16:14. These demons have been assigned by Satan to bind, possess, torment and torture people with the wicked power of darkness on the earth. However, **Satan, powers of the air, principalities, and the rulers of the darkness of this age in the heavenly places have their abode in the second heaven. God never gave His chosen people the authority or power over the evil forces of darkness in the second heaven.** If any believers raise their spiritual warfare against the higher-ranking powers of darkness in the second heavenly realms, they will be engaged in unauthorized battles without the Lord's coverings.

Therefore, Satan and his evil powers of the air can launch a counter attack against the intercessors and severely afflict them. Satan also knows the Scriptures in the Bible and what is authorized by the Lord for His children to do. After the resurrection of Jesus Christ, He declared in Matthew 28:18, *"All authority has been given to Me in heaven and on earth."* That means Jesus Christ (not His followers) has all authority over Satan and his evil powers of darkness on earth. Yet after the resurrection, Jesus Christ did not bind the devil or the powers of darkness because He could not do anything against the established will of the Father God—**Satan and his hosts of demonic powers of darkness will only be bound and cast into the abyss and the lake of fire in Rev. 20:1-3; 10** according to God's perfect will.

Let's realistically examine the fruit of spiritual warfare which focuses on binding the devil or principalities over a region, nation and city. If a believer in Christ has the delegated authority and power over Satan and His wicked hosts in heavenly places as well, then when he or she binds Satan over a city or a region or a nation, then the city or region or nation must immediately be freed from any satanic influence, power and wicked evil practices. The whole city or region or nation must experience an unprecedented revival and freedom from the power of darkness because Satan has been bound and the effect of his evil forces of darkness over the area has lost the power over people and territory. But you know that this never happens regardless of how many intercessors bind Satan as often as they can over any given area. Nevertheless, if the followers of Jesus Christ will organize mighty evangelistic forces, with signs, wonders and miracles following, to go all over a city, a region or a nation, and preach the kingdom of heaven, heal every sick person and cast demonic spirits out of anyone who had been oppressed by them, then true revival fire will fall to that territory and Satan will lose His evil power over that region.

GOD'S KINGDOM WILL NEVER BE DESTROYED

When God created Adam and Eve, He gave them two blessings: 1) they were created to live forever on the earth; 2) they received God's authority and dominion power to rule over every living thing on the earth (Genesis 1:28). However, after the fall of man, Adam and Eve forfeited their positions of authority over every living thing to the devil—he became the ruler of this world (John 12:31). Also, they lost their eternal life and men began to die from Genesis 4:8 on.

However, God didn't forget about His original plans for fallen mankind and initiated His deliverance plan in Genesis 3:15, *"And I will put enmity between you (Satan) and the woman (Israel), and between your seed and her Seed (Jesus Christ); He shall bruise (or crush) your head (Satan's head) and you shall bruise His heel."* Therefore, immediately after the fall of man, God activated His perfect deliverance plan through the chosen Seed (His own Son, Jesus Christ) in His divine time. The most important aspect of the promise of deliverance and redemption in Genesis 3:15 is that Jesus Christ would crush the head (the symbol of authority) of Satan. Jesus Christ willingly surrendered His life to be crucified on the cross in order to restore the headship to mankind that the enemy had taken from Adam. The first Adam gave up his headship by default through committing sin before the Lord. Therefore, he lost the dominion power that God had given him in Genesis 1:26.[4]

In God's perfect time, He sent His own Son (the last Adam) to die on the cross to take away the sin of the world—providing His salvation for anyone who will call upon the name of the Lord Jesus Christ. After Jesus Christ was resurrected, He sat on the throne of David to be the Ruler of this world by crushing the head of the devil as was prophesied in Isaiah 9:7, *"Of the increase of His government and peace there will be no end,* **upon the throne of David and over His kingdom***, to order it and establish it with judgment and justice from that time forward, even forever. The zeal of the Lord of hosts will perform this."*

Therefore, Jesus Christ was able to declare that all authority in heaven and on earth had been given to Him in Matthew 28:18. Jesus Christ took away the usurped authority of Satan as the ruler of this world and became the King of kings and the Lord of lords in the heavens and on earth. On the day of Pentecost, Father God and Jesus Christ sent God the Holy Spirit to be indwelt every believer in Christ. Thus, the kingdom of heaven touched down on earth. Jesus Christ, as the Last Adam, restored His kingdom authority on earth by indwelling inside of every believer to exercise His authority on earth through him or her. Also, He sent the Holy Spirit to empower the followers of Christ with His kingdom power to destroy the works of the devil (1 John 3:8). Jesus Christ brought the kingdom of heaven down to the earth to expand

His kingdom rule over every nation, people, tongue and tribe according to Matthew 24:14:

> *And this gospel of the kingdom will be preached in all the world as a witness to all the nations* (*ethne: all the families of the earth*), *and then the end will come.*

Therefore, the kingdom of heaven that has been activated on the earth through the Holy Spirit indwelling believers in Christ cannot be destroyed, because it came down from God in heaven as described in John 18:36, *"My kingdom is not of this world. If My kingdom were of this world, My servants would fight, so that I should not be delivered to the Jews; but now My kingdom is not from here."*

The kingdom of heaven is wherever the reign or dominion of God is manifested. The Father demonstrated His kingdom power through Moses to the Egyptian kingdom in Exodus. Jesus Christ performed many signs, wonders and miracles which are recorded in the four gospels. The Holy Spirit continuously demonstrates the kingdom power through disciples of Christ by setting people free from the power of Satan. Thus, God's kingdom on earth will never be destroyed until Revelation 11:15b is fulfilled, *"The kingdoms of this world have become the kingdoms of our Lord and of His Christ, and He shall reign forever and ever!"*

Since the day of Pentecost, God has sent His Spirit to create living temples of the Holy Spirit from Jerusalem, Judea, Samaria, and the ends of the earth. In reality, Jesus Christ has been multiplied through the Holy Spirit over billions of His disciples from Jerusalem to every people, tribe, tongue and nation to fulfill the prophecy in Matthew 24:14. The Roman Empire tried to destroy the kingdom of heaven on earth, but she eventually bowed her knees to Jesus Christ. Communism tried to destroy God's kingdom on earth, but it has been diminished and the gospel has been preached to most of the former Communist countries. Now radical Islamic forces are trying to destroy God's kingdom on earth, but we know, according to His prophecies to Daniel, that Islamic power will be destroyed sooner or later. God's kingdom will never be destroyed:

> *And in the days of these kings the God of heaven will set up a kingdom which shall never be destroyed; and the kingdom shall not be left to other people; it shall break in pieces and consume all these kingdoms, and it shall stand forever.* (Daniel 2:44)

> *And behold, One like the Son of Man, coming with the clouds of heaven! He came to the Ancient of Days, and they brought Him near before Him. Then to Him was given dominion and glory and a kingdom, that all peoples, nations, and languages should serve Him. His dominion is an everlasting dominion, which shall not pass away, and His kingdom the one which shall not be destroyed.* (Daniel 7:13-14)

TOTALLY DEPENDING ON GOD FOR SPIRITUAL WARFARE

Once we understand God is in absolute control over the whole universe, we can totally trust Him and ask Him through prayers and supplications to help us in times of our struggles, sufferings, temptations, persecutions, sicknesses, distress and financial difficulties. God always hears our sincere prayers that have been rendered to Him with a contrite and broken spirit. When we go through difficult times in life, the devil will come and cause us to doubt God's power, authority, love, mercy, grace and faithfulness. During our most vulnerable times, the devil will cause us to launch spiritual warfare directly against him so that he can draw us away from totally relying on God to overcome the battle. The devil wants us to behave as though we can be our own gods to know good and evil for ourselves without depending on God for everything. Self-righteousness, self-reliance and self-wisdom all come from the pride of life and they will always lead us away from the truth, wisdom, guidance and power of God.

When we know that God is in absolute control over the affairs of the whole universe, it is very simple for His children to focus on God when dealing with any spiritual warfare that we might face during the journey of this short life on the earth. **The biblically correct method of spiritual warfare is not to focus on Satan and demonic powers of darkness, but to trust the Lord for His mighty power to deliver us from any wicked schemes of the enemy.** Jesus Christ won total victory over Satan and all the powers of darkness once and forever at the cross and He was resurrected by the power of the Holy Spirit (Romans 8:11).

Therefore, we don't need to fight for our own victory against the power of the enemy, but we fight from the victory that Jesus Christ won at the cross. He conquered the five aspects of the works of the devil on the cross—(1) power of sin: John 1:29; (2) sicknesses: 1 Peter 2:24; (3) curses: Galatians 3:13-14; (4) fear of death: Hebrews 2:14-15; 1 Corinthians 15:54-57; and (5) Satan: Genesis 3:15; 1 John 3:8b.

God created human beings to resemble the image and likeness of the triune God. All other existing beings and things in the heavens and the earth were created by the word of God. He said in Genesis 1:3, *"'Let there be light'; and there was light."* He said in Genesis 1:20, *"Let the waters abound with an abundance of living creatures, and let birds fly above the earth across the face of the firmament of the heavens."* As God spoke, those beings came into existence according to His commands. However, when He created man, He created him out of the dust of the ground according to Genesis 2:7, *"And the Lord God formed man of the dust of the ground, and breathed into his nostrils the breath of life; and man became a living being."* God created man in His own image; in the image of God He created him; male and female, He created them (Genesis 1:27). Therefore, men were created to talk, act and live like their Creator by putting their absolute trust in Him.

Chapter 3

SATAN HAS ALREADY BEEN DEFEATED

In this chapter, we will examine the origin of Satan, his downfall, his method of deception, his evil schemes against human beings and his final judgment in the lake of fire. As we examine the beginning and the end of Satan's fate in the Bible, we will fully realize that God is absolutely in control over all the affairs of the heavens and the earth. Satan was a created angelic being who had been condemned and cast out of heaven by God when sin was discovered in him. After the devil had been cast out of heaven into the earth, he deceived Adam and Eve to sin against God's command in Genesis 2:16-17 so that the judgment of death would fall upon them and all of their descendants.

After the fall of man, Satan usurped man's authority to have dominion over every living thing on the earth (Genesis 1:28) and he became the ruler of the world according to John 14:30, *"I will no longer talk much with you, for the ruler of this world is coming, and he has nothing in Me."* Furthermore, Adam and Eve and their descendants, who were originally created to live forever on the earth, began to die. The first man ever to die on earth was Abel who was killed by his own brother, Cain in Genesis 4:8. Consequently, mankind lost two blessings of God: 1) **Eternal life** on the earth; 2) **Dominion**

power to rule over the affairs of the earth. Ever since the fall of man, Satan has been deceiving as many human beings as he can to take them to hell and eventually to the eternal lake of fire with him. However, God hasn't forgotten His original plans for mankind. So, He has initiated His divine deliverance plan to save as many human beings as possible by providing eternal life back to His chosen children and restoring His Kingdom authority and power for those who obey His commandments.

THE INITIAL DELIVERANCE PLAN

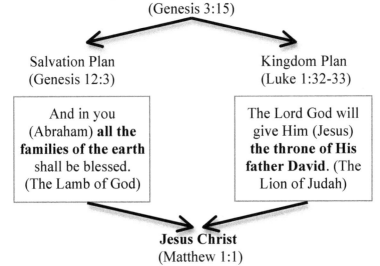

"And I will put enmity between you (Satan) *and the woman* (Israel) *and between your seed and her Seed* (Jesus Christ); *He shall bruise your head, and you shall bruise His heel."*
(Genesis 3:15)

Salvation Plan
(Genesis 12:3)

Kingdom Plan
(Luke 1:32-33)

And in you (Abraham) **all the families of the earth** shall be blessed. (The Lamb of God)

The Lord God will give Him (Jesus) **the throne of His father David.** (The Lion of Judah)

Jesus Christ
(Matthew 1:1)
Fulfillment: *"The Son of David & the Son of Abraham"*
(**Jesus Christ:** *The Lion and the Lamb of God*)

The first Adam had miserably failed God's divine plan for mankind and lost His appointed blessings and position of authority to the devil (Genesis 3:1-6). Therefore, God sent His own Son (the Son of God), Jesus Christ, as the last Adam (the Son of Man), into the world to restore what the first Adam had lost to His chosen people—believers in Christ. In order for Jesus Christ to come as the Messiah not only for the Israelites but also for the Gentiles of the world, He had to come to fulfill two plans of God: 1) **Salvation Plan**—as **the son of Abraham (the Lamb of God)** to die on the cross to take away the sin of the world in order to restore eternal life back to His chosen people—the Jews and the Gentile believers of Yeshua Hamashiach (Jesus the Messiah: John 3:16); 2) **Kingdom Plan**—as **the son of David (the Lion of Judah),** He was resurrected to sit on the throne of His father David to restore Kingdom authority and power back to His chosen people on the earth, so they can fulfill the promise of Matthew 24:14 with signs, wonders and miracles following (Matthew 10:7-8):

> *And this gospel of the kingdom will be preached in all the world as a witness to all the nations, and then the end will come.* (Matthew 24:14)

> *And as you go, preach, saying, 'The kingdom of heaven is at hand.' Heal the sick, cleanse the lepers, raise the dead, cast out demons. Freely you have received, freely give.* (Matthew 10:7-8)

SALVATION PLAN

God originally created the Israelites to be a missionary nation to all the families of the earth (the Gentiles) according to Genesis 12:3. Eventually, Jesus Christ the Messiah would be born through woman (the nation of Israel) as the Lamb of God to take away the sin of the world (John 1:29). Therefore, Jesus Christ declared in John 3:16, *"For God so loved the world that He gave His only begotten Son, that whoever believes in Him should not perish but have **everlasting life**."* Also, we can identify the heart of God for the lost in the world in 2 Peter 3:9, *"The Lord is not slack concerning His promise, as some count slackness, but is longsuffering toward us, not willing that any should perish but that all should come to repentance."*

God's desire is for all the families of the earth to hear the gospel and be saved (Matthew 24:14). According to the Joshua Project (www.joshuaproject.net), there are still over 7,000 Unreached People Groups (UPGs) in the world. When the last UPG hears the gospel of the kingdom of heaven, then the end will come—Jesus Christ will come back as the King of kings and the Lord of lords to rule and reign on the earth with all His saints (1 Thessalonians 3:13).

KINGDOM PLAN

Jesus Christ died on the cross as the Lamb of God to take away the sin of the world, but He was resurrected as the Lion of Judah to sit on the throne of His father David as the last Adam to establish the kingdom of God on the earth to destroy the works of the devil (1 John 3:8b). In order for the message of the kingdom of God to be proclaimed from Jerusalem to the end of the earth (Acts 1:8), Jesus Christ, the Last Adam took away the usurped authority of Satan (Matthew 28:18-20) and made it available for His born-again children of God by living inside of them (Matthew 14:20):

> *And Jesus came and spoke to them, saying, "**All authority has been given to Me in heaven and on***

earth. *Go therefore and make disciples of all the nations, baptizing them in the name of the Father and of the Son and of the Holy Spirit, teaching them to observe all things that I have commanded you; and lo, I am with you always, even to the end of the age." Amen.* (Matthew 28:18-20)

*At that day you will know that I am in My Father, and **you in Me, and I in you.*** (John 14:20)

    Jesus Christ, the last Adam, as the perfect Son of Man received all authority in heaven and on earth. As Jesus indwells believers, He can release His authority to them to fulfill the will of Father God on earth. With that authority, believers can go into all the world to make disciples of Christ. However, for the disciples to just have the delegated authority of Christ was not enough; they also needed the power of the Holy Spirit to expand God's kingdom plan from Jerusalem to the end of the earth according to Acts 1:8, "*But **you shall receive power when the Holy Spirit has come upon you**; and you shall be witnesses to Me in Jerusalem, and in all Judea and Samaria, and to the end of the earth.*"

    Therefore, the initial 120 disciples had to wait upon the Lord for the outpouring of His Spirit upon them on the day of Pentecost—the day God's Kingdom Plan was reinitiated on the earth. Then they began to move in Christ's authority and the power of the Holy Spirit to evangelize the UPGs and to destroy the works of the devil with accompanying signs, wonders and miracles.

    The result was that the disciples of Christ moved with the Salvation Plan to save as many souls as they could wherever they went. And they demonstrated the Kingdom Plan to heal the sick, cast out demons, cleanse lepers and raise the dead in the name of Jesus Christ. Satan's head had been crushed when

Jesus Christ was raised from the dead. Satan's days are numbered as the kingdom of God advances from Jerusalem to the end of the earth. When the last UPG hears the gospel of the kingdom of God, Jesus Christ will come back and the prophesy of Revelation 7:9-10 will be fulfilled:

> *After these things I looked, and behold, a great multitude which no one could number, of **all nations, tribes, peoples, and tongues, standing before the throne and before the Lamb**, clothed with white robes, with palm branches in their hands, and crying out with a loud voice, saying, "Salvation belongs to our God who sits on the throne, and to the Lamb!*

THE ORIGIN OF SATAN

Satan, who was called "Lucifer" and one of the archangels in heaven, possessed great wisdom, power, beauty, and perfection when God created him. Lucifer might have been one of the highest-ranking archangels serving in the presence of God having co-equal power with archangels Michael and Gabriel. He was also called "the anointed cherub" who directly attended to God in Ezekiel 28:14 and as "son of the morning" or "morning star" in Isaiah 14:12.

The important fact is that Lucifer was a created angelic being in heaven before the fall. However, after the fall, Lucifer came to be recognized as the great dragon, the serpent of old, the devil and Satan (Revelation 12:9). As a created angelic being, Satan is no match for the Creator God, Jesus Christ and the Holy Spirit. Before the fall of Lucifer, God recognized him as perfect in his ways from the day he was created, till iniquity was found in him:

You were the seal of perfection, full of wisdom and perfect in beauty. You were in Eden, the garden of God...You were the anointed cherub who covers; I established you; You were on the holy mountain of God...You were perfect in your ways from the day you were created, till iniquity was found in you.
(Ezekiel 28:12b, 13a, 14a, 15)

According to the above Scriptures, it is very clear that God created Lucifer as an archangel perfect in beauty and full of wisdom to glorify Him as His servant. He was allowed to be on the holy mountain of God and to guard the Garden of Eden. Until iniquity was found in Lucifer, God considered him to be perfect in all his ways. What a great honor Lucifer had from God before the fall!

THE FALL OF LUCIFER

We may wonder how a perfect angel like Lucifer could have fallen from the glory of the Lord! Well, God gave all His created angels and human beings their own freewill to choose. Freely obeying and serving the Lord according to His perfect ways and commandments would cause them to fully enjoy His perfect blessings. However, disobeying and rejecting His ways and creation mandates would cause them to fall away from His presence, glory and blessed purpose. Unfortunately, Lucifer chose to rebel against the Creator God, as did Adam and Eve, and fell from the glory of God. The Scriptures describe the reasons why Lucifer was cast out from heaven in Ezekiel 28:16-19:

You became filled with violence within, and you sinned; therefore I cast you as a profane thing out of the mountain of God; and I destroyed you, O covering cherub, from the midst of the fiery stones. ***Your heart was lifted up because of your beauty; you corrupted your wisdom for the sake of your splendor;*** *I cast you to the ground, I laid you before kings, that they might gaze at you.* ***You defiled your sanctuaries by the multitude of your iniquities****, by the iniquity of your trading; therefore I brought fire from your midst; it devoured you, and I turned you to ashes upon the earth in the sight of all who saw you. All who knew you among the peoples are astonished at you;* ***you have become a horror, and shall be no more forever.***

Let's examine the above statements of God against Lucifer:

- You became filled with **violence within and you sinned**: Obviously after Lucifer decided to rebel against God, he began to fill himself with violence (Hebrew [*chamas*]: malicious, violence, turbulent wrong; intense, or furious and often destructive action or force) or violent ways and means to commit sin before the Creator God. Since being cast down into the earth, Satan hasn't changed his tactics against the apex of God's creation—human beings. According to John 10:10a, *"The thief (Satan) does not come except to steal, and to kill, and to destroy."* From the beginning, one of Satan's main tools has been violence.

    Therefore, the children of God must not allow themselves to be influenced by the devil to engage in defaming other ministers; in speaking malicious words against anyone with whom they don't agree; or in falsely accusing others such that their reputations can be destroyed.

- **I cast you as a profane** (Hebrew [*chalal*]: polluted, profaned, defiled or violated) **thing out of the mountain of God:** Once Lucifer was the most beautiful and perfect angel in heaven; however, when he sinned within his heart, God cast him as a profane thing (like a garbage bag filled with filthy things) out of the mountain of God. Satan was immediately judged and condemned by the Creator God and such a defiled thing couldn't stay in the presence of the holy and pure living God any longer.

  Therefore, we can see God is in charge over the fate of Lucifer from the beginning of his fall until the final judgment against him to be carried out in Revelation 20:10, *"The devil, who deceived them, was cast into the lake of fire and brimstone where the beast and the false prophet are. And they will be tormented day and night forever and ever."* Likewise, sons and daughters of God must not take part in anything that can be considered by the Holy Spirit as profaned, defiled and violated things of the devil.

- **Your heart was lifted up because of your beauty:** Lucifer must have been one of the most beautiful archangels in heaven before the fall. Because of his own beauty, he became very proud of himself without realizing or honoring the fact that it was God who created him to be beautiful. Therefore the Word of God warns against a prideful spirit in Proverb 16:18, *"Pride goes before destruction, and a haughty spirit before a fall."* Also, in James 4:6, *"God resists the proud, but gives grace to the humble."*

  The ultimate reason for Satan's fall was his prideful spirit that tried to exalt himself above the Creator God. Therefore, the children of God also must humble themselves before Him when His blessings are abundantly flowing into their lives. They must not credit their successes to their own wisdom, ways, knowledge, and beauties or exalt themselves.

- **You corrupted your wisdom for the sake of your splendor:** Satan obviously had God ordained wisdom to manage heavenly affairs under the command of the Creator. However, when Satan was filled with his own beauty and pride, he began to corrupt his divine wisdom to carry out his own wicked plans against the will of God. God given wisdom and splendor must only be used to accomplish His will and for His glory alone.

  I also have witnessed many successful ministers fall from their positions of glory when they began to corrupt their Holy Spirit ordained gifts and blessings in order to carry out their own wicked plans against the will of God. I know of one brother who was a converted believer of Christ from the Islamic faith in Ethiopia. He became a born-again believer when he encountered Jesus Christ while he was clinically dead.

  When he came back to life, he received God's supernatural healing anointing. He led many people to the Lord and performed many miracles in His name and eventually he became well known in Ethiopia. However, he became very proud and began to misuse God's funds and abuse His workers. He didn't humble himself and listen to other pastors' advice and warnings for some time. One day, though young and healthy, he suddenly died. His prideful, arrogant heart and misusing the gifts of the Holy Spirit for his own glory caused his own destruction.

- **I cast you to the ground:** The Lord judged Satan and cast him to the ground (to the earth). Therefore, it was God who rendered His sentence against rebellious Satan who had committed sin before Him in heaven. God can do whatever He chooses with His created beings in heaven and on earth according to the written words in the Bible. Also, Satan has already been condemned to be cast into the lake of fire in the future according to Revelation 20:10. Until then, Satan has his appointed time by God to operate his wicked evil schemes against human beings on earth. So the Scripture in Revelation 12:12 states, *"Woe to the inhabitants of the earth and the sea! For the devil has come down to you, having great wrath, because **he knows that he has a short time**."*

Since the devil knows that he has a short time left on the earth, he has been warring against God's chosen people according to Revelation 12:17, *"And the dragon was enraged with the woman* (Israel), *and he went to make war with **the rest of her offspring, who keep the commandments of God** (the Jews) **and have the testimony of Jesus Christ** (Christians)."* Unfortunately, there will be worldwide persecution of Jews and Christians prior to the second coming of Christ. Currently, there are more than 215 million persecuted Christians worldwide, according to the 2018 "World Watch List."

Therefore, sons and daughters of God must prepare their hearts to face the persecution of the devil as His anointed warriors to fulfill the prophetic word of the Apostle John in Revelation 12:11, *"And they overcame him (Satan) by the blood of the Lamb and by the word of their testimony, and they did not love their lives to the death."*

- **You defiled your sanctuaries by the multitude of your iniquities:** Sanctuary (Hebrew [*miqdash*]: holy place, sacred part, a consecrated place where sacred objects are kept). Satan began to defile his assigned domain in heaven by the multitude of his iniquities. The Bible doesn't describe what kinds of specific iniquities Satan committed within God's holy places, but we can suspect that he was setting himself above God's rules and commandments in heaven.

For children of God, our bodies are the temples of the Holy Spirit—God's holy sanctuary on the earth. Therefore, we must not defile our bodies because they belong to the Lord according to 1 Corinthians 6:19-20, *"Or do you not know that **your body is the temple of the Holy Spirit** who is in you, whom you have from God, and you are not your own? **For you were bought at a price (the blood of the Lamb of God)**; therefore glorify God in your body and in your spirit, which are God's."*

- **I turned you to ashes upon the earth…you have become a horror, and shall be no more forever:** It was the most horrifying judgment that Satan could ever receive from the almighty living God. Once he was the most beautiful, wise, splendid and beloved cherub or archangel in heaven, but God cast him down to the earth and he would eventually fall into the lake of fire to become ashes and a profane thing forever. Sadly, Satan became a disobedient, rebellious, violent, prideful, arrogant, miserable, rejected and profane orphan who had been cast from his eternal home in heaven down into the earth.

Now he is waiting to receive his final judgment of God to fall into the eternal lake of fire in the near future. Therefore, we, the children of God, must not allow Satan to have any part in us by not yielding to his temptations. We must walk in the Spirit so that we will not fulfill the lust of the flesh (Galatians 5:16). If the Holy Spirit has all of us, then Satan will not have any part in us. Jesus Christ has given us His life and that life imparts to us freedom in Him so that we can move like the wind of the Holy Spirit to destroy the works of the devil.

Since Lucifer committed sins before the presence of God, His judgment fell on him. Therefore, God cast him as a profane thing out of the mountain of God. That means, God immediately judged Lucifer as soon as he committed sin before Him and he was treated as a dirty and unholy thing to be thrown out of heaven. Lucifer became very proud of himself because of his natural beauty and splendor, instead of giving God the glory for his marvelous wisdom and appearance.

Ultimately, Lucifer defiled his sanctuaries (dwelling place, domain of authority or sphere of influence) by the multitude of his iniquities by the sin of his trading (possibly dealing with other angelic beings under his authority). The final judgment has already been rendered to Lucifer as God declared, *"**you have become a horror, and shall be no more forever***" (either in heaven or on earth). Eventually, Lucifer, his fallen angels and disobedient human beings will be cast into the lake of fire forever and ever (Revelation 20:10, 15). Therefore, we absolutely need to understand that God has already judged Lucifer from the moment he sinned before God in heaven. A created angelic being, Lucifer was and is and always will be no match for the mighty Creator God who rules the whole affairs of the universe with His divine power.

YOU SHALL BE BROUGHT DOWN TO SHEOL

Lucifer's five *"I will"* statements, spoken in his heart before he even uttered any one of them aloud, caused him to fall from the glory of God. That means while Lucifer was simply thinking about them in his heart, God already knew what he was planning and He pronounced His judgment against him. Even now, omnipotent, omniscient and omnipresent God knows exactly what His heavenly angels, every human being, fallen angels and Satan are thinking about in their hearts. Lucifer's five "*I will*" statements that caused his downfall are written in Isaiah 14:12-15:

> *How you are fallen from heaven, O Lucifer, son of the morning! How you are cut down to the ground, you who weakened the nations!* **For you have said in your heart:** *'**I will** ascend into heaven,* **I will** *exalt my throne above the stars of God;* **I will** *also sit on the mount of the congregation on the farthest sides of the north;* **I will** *ascend above the heights of the clouds,* **I will** *be like the Most High.' Yet you shall be brought down to Sheol, to the lowest depths of the Pit.*

When Lucifer said in his heart five "I will" statements, God already knew his evil intentions:

1) **I will** ascend into heaven—it can be interpreted that he wanted to raise his influence above the level and authority of the Creator God.

2) **I will** exalt my throne above the stars of God—it is more obvious that he wanted to exalt his authority to rule the heaven above any of God's angels.

3) **I will** also sit on the mount of the congregation on the farthest sides of the north—Lucifer wanted to be seated in the highest places in the north to rule the whole congregation of the inhabitants of heaven.

4) **I will** ascend above the heights of the clouds—Lucifer desired to expand his dominion beyond the heights of the clouds (glory) of God in heaven.

5) **I will** be like the Most High—it is clear that Lucifer understood that he could never say he would be the Most High because he knew he was a created angelic being. So, he could only say that he would wish to be like the Most High God, the Creator.

As soon as God perceived Lucifer's five *"I will"* intentions in his heart, He pronounced His judgment against him by saying; *"you shall be brought down to Sheol* (the abode of the dead: Psalm 88:3, 5; in the New Testament: Hades—a place of torment) *to the lowest depths of the Pit."* That means God knows every intention of Satan's wicked plans he is contemplating in his heart. God is absolutely in control over Satan and I believe almighty God uses him to fulfill His divine plan on the earth. God is the Alpha and the Omega, the beginning and the end. Ultimately, Satan will be thrown into the eternal lake of fire in the near future. Therefore, we need to fear the Lord as Jesus Christ taught in Luke 12:4-5:

> *And I say to you, My friends, do not be afraid of those who kill the body, and after that have no more that they can do. But I will show you whom you should fear:* **Fear Him who, after He has killed, has power to cast into hell***; yes, I say to you, fear Him!*

As the Church of the living God fears the Lord and not the devil and his wicked evil power of darkness, then His name will be glorified as Psalmist declared in Psalm 33:8, *"Let all the earth fear the Lord; Let all the inhabitants of the world stand in awe of Him."* The Lord will fight the battles for the one who fears Him and stands in awe of Him.

SATAN WAS CAST TO THE EARTH

We do not know exactly when Lucifer was cast down to the earth and became Satan. As we examine Revelation 12, we will be able to discover the events that took place in heaven and on earth in regards to the fall of Satan:

> *Now a great sign appeared in heaven:* ***a woman clothed with the sun, with the moon under her feet, and on her head a garland of twelve stars.*** *Then being with child, she cried out in labor and in pain to give birth. And another sign appeared in heaven: behold,* ***a great, fiery red dragon*** *having seven heads and ten horns, and seven diadems on his heads.* ***His tail drew a third of the stars of heaven and threw them to the earth.*** *And the dragon stood before the woman who was ready to give birth, to devour her Child as soon as it was born.* ***She bore a male Child who was to rule all nations*** *with a rod of iron. And* ***her Child was caught up to God and His throne.*** *Then the woman fled into the wilderness, where she has a place prepared by God, that they should feed her there* ***one thousand two hundred and sixty days.*** *And war broke out in heaven;* ***Michael and his angels fought against the dragon;*** *and the dragon and his angels fought, but they did not prevail, nor was a place found for them in heaven any longer. So* ***the great dragon*** *was cast out, that* ***serpent of old,*** *called the* ***Devil and Satan,*** *who deceives the*

whole world; he was cast to the earth, and his angels were cast out with him. (Revelation 12:1-9)

Let us examine the above Scriptures one section at a time:

- *"a woman clothed with the sun, with the moon under her feet, and on her head a garland of twelve stars"*: The woman can be recognized as the nation of Israel who brought forth Jesus Christ as the Savior of the world. Abraham, Isaac and Jacob produced the twelve tribes (*twelve stars*) of the Israelites that had become the chosen seeds of God. Eventually, in God's perfect time, Jesus Christ, the Messiah of the Jews and the Gentiles of the world, would be born as **the Son of David (a tribe of Judah) and the Son of Abraham** (Matthew 1:1 – the first verse of the New Testament).

- *"a great, fiery red dragon having seven heads and ten horns, and seven diadems on his heads. His tail drew a third of the stars of heaven and threw them to the earth"*: The great fiery red dragon was fallen Lucifer who became Satan and he drew a third of the stars of heaven and threw them to the earth as he was cast out of heaven. According to these Scriptures, it is clear that Lucifer, somehow, enticed one third of the angels that were probably under his command in heaven, to rebel together with him against God and they were also cast down to the earth. One third of the fallen angels became principalities, powers, the rulers of the darkness of this age, spiritual hosts of wickedness and demons (Ephesians 6:12).

- *"And the dragon stood before the woman who was ready to give birth, to devour her Child as soon as it was born"*: The Child is the Son of the living God, Jesus Christ. Satan tried to kill the Child by enticing king Herod to kill all the male children who were in Bethlehem and in all its districts from two years old and under, according to Matthew 2:1-18.

- *"She bore a male Child who was to rule all nations with a rod of iron. And her Child was caught up to God and His throne"*: The male Child, Jesus Christ—the Messiah of the world, will ultimately rule all nations with His divine power when He comes back again in the near future. However, when He first came to the earth He was to die on the cross to take away the sin of the world to provide God's salvation to as many souls as He could from Jerusalem to the end of the earth. After His resurrection, He ascended to God and His throne in heaven and became the King of kings and the Lord of lords.

- *"Then the woman fled into the wilderness, where she has a place prepared by God, that they should feed her there one thousand two hundred and sixty days"*: One thousand two hundred and sixty days are equal to three and a half years, the same amount of time as Jesus Christ's time of ministry on the earth. In a short one thousand two hundred and sixty days, Jesus Christ accomplished all of the Father's missions to provide the Salvation and the Kingdom plans for fallen mankind as the last Adam.

- *"And war broke out in heaven; Michael and his angels fought against the dragon; and the dragon and his angels fought, but they did not prevail, nor was a place found for them in heaven any longer"*: Ultimately, the archangel Michael and his angels fought against the dragon (Lucifer) and his angels and they were finally cast out of heaven forever. From that time on, Lucifer became the orphan Satan who came down to the earth to manipulate, deceive, lie and torment God's created human beings to follow his wicked schemes on the earth with the assistance of his fallen angels (demons).

- *"So the great dragon was cast out, that serpent of old, called the Devil and Satan, who deceives the whole world; he was cast to the earth, and his angels were cast out with him"*: In this Scripture, we can identify the four nicknames of Lucifer as the great dragon, the serpent of old, the Devil and Satan. His main schemes on the earth have been to deceive the whole world by empowering his political, religious, ideological and social leaders of the nations to adhere to his wicked evil schemes to hinder the works of the kingdom of God.

For example, Satan used the Roman Empire to persecute and murder as many Christians as possible for over 300 years since the birth of the New Testament Church in Jerusalem. In the 20th century, Satan created and used Communism to destroy as many Christians as possible throughout the world for 70 years (still the same persecution is going on in North Korea, China, Cuba, Vietnam and several other Communist countries). Ever since the birth of Islam around 600 A.D., the Islamic power has been trying very hard to destroy Jews and Christians.

But the Bible declares in Revelation 11:15, *"The kingdoms of this world have become the kingdoms of our Lord and of His Christ, and He shall reign forever and ever!"* Also, Daniel 2:44 declares, *"And in the days of these kings the God of heaven will set up a kingdom which shall never be destroyed."*

SATAN KNOWS THAT HE HAS A SHORT TIME

We can examine the rest of the Scriptures in Revelation Chapter 12 and discover Satan's plots on the earth with his limited time left:

> "Then I heard a loud voice saying in heaven, "Now salvation, and strength, and **the kingdom of our God, and the power of His Christ have come**, for the accuser of our brethren, who accused them before our God day and night, has been cast down. **And they overcame him by the blood of the Lamb and by the word of their testimony**, and they did not love their lives to the death. Therefore rejoice, O heavens, and you who dwell in them! **Woe to the inhabitants of the earth** and the sea! For the devil has come down to you, having great wrath, because he knows that **he has a short time**. (Revelation 12:10-12)

Let us examine the above Scriptures to discover Satan's evil schemes on the earth:

- *"Then I heard a loud voice saying in heaven, "Now **salvation, and strength, and the kingdom of our God, and the power of His Christ have come**, for the accuser of our brethren, who accused them before our God day and night, has been cast down"*: After the resurrection of Christ, the kingdom of our God and the power of His Christ have come to the inhabitants of the earth. However, in Old Testament days, Satan was able to go up to the presence of God according to Job 1:6-7, *"Now there was a day when the sons of God came to present themselves* *before the Lord, and Satan also came among them. And the Lord said to Satan, 'From where do you come?' So Satan answered the Lord and said, 'From going to and fro on the earth, and from walking back and forth on it.'"* In this context, it is obvious that Satan had been cast down to the earth already; however, he was able to come up to present himself before God.

Nevertheless, I believe that, following the resurrection of Jesus Christ, Satan has no longer been allowed to come up and present himself before God. Since then, Jesus Christ declared, *"All authority has been given to Me in heaven and on earth."* (Matthew 28:18). Therefore, Satan has lost any authority he had in heaven and on earth.

- *"And **they overcame him by the blood of the Lamb and by the word of their testimony**, and they did not love their lives to the death. Therefore rejoice, O heavens, and you who dwell in them!"*: No matter how viciously Satan tried to terminate believers in Christ following the day of Pentecost, they were able to prevail by the blood of the Lamb and their living testimonies of victory in Christ. The sacrificial death of Christ on the cross set the chosen people of God free from the power of sin, sickness, curses, the fear of death and Satan himself. Therefore, the blood of martyrs paved the way for God's church to rise up through the power of the Holy Spirit from Jerusalem to the end of the earth (Acts 1:8).

- *"Woe to the inhabitants of the earth and the sea! For the devil has come down to you, having great wrath, because **he knows that he has a short time**"*: Now Satan has been cast down to the earth and he knows that he has a limited time left before he will be cast into the lake of fire. Therefore, Satan is furious, knowing his doomed fate so he has been unleashing his great wrath and deceptions on the inhabitants of the earth by enticing them to believe his false ideologies, religions, philosophies, and belief systems. The ultimate goal of Satan is to take as many people as he can with him to the eternal lake of fire.

SATAN PERSECUTES THE JEWS AND CHRISTIANS

Satan has been persecuting Jews and Christians throughout the history of mankind because they are God's chosen people. Now we can further examine Satan's intentions against Jews and Christians according to God's Scriptures:

> *Now when the dragon saw that he had been cast to the earth, **he persecuted the woman who gave birth to the male Child**. But the woman was given two wings of a great eagle, that she might fly into the wilderness to her place, where she is nourished for a time and times and half a time, from the presence of the serpent...And the dragon was enraged with the woman, and **he went to make war with the rest of her offspring, who keep the commandments of God and have the testimony of Jesus Christ**.* (Revelation 12:13-17)

Since Satan knows that he has a short time, he has great wrath against God's chosen people. Satan persecuted the woman (Israel) who gave birth to the male Child (Jesus Christ) and then made war with **the rest of her offspring (the Jews), who keep the commandments of God**. Throughout the history of the Jewish people, Satan has continuously enticed the leaders of the nations to persecute the Jews. The book of Esther describes the evil plots of Haman against the Jews during the King Ahasuerus's rule over Persia and Media. Unfortunately, more than six million Jews were terminated in Europe under the control of Nazi Party in Germany during the World War II.

Not only that, ever since the birth of the first church in Jerusalem, Satan has been furious, destroying **Christians who have the testimony of Jesus Christ**. Satan has been trying by every possible means to persecute Christians for the past 2,000 years. There have been persecutions against Christians by the Roman Empire, Persian and Median Empires, the Ottoman Empire and other Islamic powers, radical Hindus and Buddhists, and Communist powers. Most recently, ISIS' (Islamic State of Iraq and Syria) has killed many Christians in Iraq and Syria. Unfortunately, there will be greater persecutions against Christians worldwide before the second coming of Christ.

Regardless of Satan's persecutions of Jews and Christians, the Church of the living God has been continuously growing in the world—the blood of martyrs is the seed of the church. For example, in the beginning of the Communist rule in China in 1949, there were approximately one million Christians. However, Professor Fenggang Yang of Purdue University stated that approximately 100 - 130 million Christians were in China in 2010. Christianity has been rapidly growing for the past 30 years not only in China, but also in many other parts of Asia, all over Africa, Central and South America and Middle Eastern countries.

Satan knows his fate and he especially understands when the end will come for him according to Matthew 24:14, *"And **this gospel of the kingdom will be preached in all the world** as a witness to **all the nations** [Greek: ethne—every people group]*, *and then the end will come."* Every people, tongue, tribe and nation must hear the gospel in order for Jesus Christ to come back. Therefore, Satan is trying to do everything possible in his power for Matthew 24:14 not to be fulfilled for a long time by deceiving as many people groups as he can with false religious belief systems, ideologies, political and social barriers, etc.

Joshua Project states that there are still over 7,000 Unreached People Groups (UPGs) in the world. If the Church of the living God will use all of her efforts, resources and energies to evangelize the remaining UPGs in this generation, then the end will come in the near future. Sons and daughters of God must make the Great Commission become the Great Completion as quickly as possible so they can further shorten the remaining time of Satan on the earth. Then, Jesus Christ will come back and cast Satan into the bottomless pit and He will rule and reign on the earth with His Saints for a thousand years (Revelation 20:2-4).

PERSECUTION OF CHRISTIANS

Let's discuss more about the persecution of Christians. The first three hundred years of church history, the Roman Empire tried to destroy God's kingdom on earth by killing as many Christians as it could. However, gradually, the Roman Empire became Christianized after the Edict of Milan in 313 AD. Over the past 2,000 years, many different religions, empires, ideologies and kingdoms of the world have persecuted Christians throughout the world. The Persian Sassanid Empire massacred over a thousand Christians in 341 AD. Also, when Persia conquered Jerusalem in 614 AD, the siege resulted in a Christian death toll of 17,000. The persecution of Christians under Islamic rule has been ongoing since the mid-7th century AD. For example, the Adana massacre occurred under the Ottoman Empire in 1909 and over 30,000 Armenian and Assyrian Christians were killed. Even today, thousands of Christians in Iraq and Syria have become martyrs under the rule of ISIS. No one knows, how many millions of Christians have been killed under the Islamic rules worldwide.

Millions of Christians have become martyrs under the communist controlled Soviet Union, Eastern European countries, China, Cambodia, Vietnam, North Korea, Cuba and many African countries. Also, radical Hindus and Buddhists attacked and killed numerous Christians over the past 2,000 years. Between 1603 AD and 1639 AD, over 200,000 Catholic believers were martyred in Japan.[4]

According to the Joshua Project (www.joshuaproject.net), more Christians were martyred in the 20th century than in the previous 19 centuries combined. About 200 million Christians in 60 countries currently suffer persecution. Globally, approximately one in ten Christians suffers persecution. Every 24 hours, another 480 believers are martyred for their faith in Christ. However, according to the Word of God in Daniel 2:44b, *"it (the Kingdom of God) shall break in pieces and consume all these kingdoms, and it shall stand forever,"* the Kingdom of God (God's living temples of the Holy Spirit or the Church of the living God—that the author calls as "the Kingdom Stations on the earth") will never be destroyed.

If we examine the world history, the Roman Empire, Persian Empire, Ottoman Empire, most of the Communist countries and any other forces that have risen up against the Kingdom of God have either been destroyed or vanished. Eventually, Creator God will consume all the kingdoms of the world according to Revelation 11:15. Also, the prophesy of Daniel 7:27a will be fulfilled in the future, *"Then the kingdom and dominion, and the greatness of the kingdoms under the whole heaven, shall be given to the people, the saints of the Most High."*

SATAN AND DEMONS HAVE AN APPOINTED TIME ON THE EARTH

Throughout the four gospels we see Jesus Christ cast many demons out of people who had been tormented by them. In the book of Acts, we see the apostles doing the same. When Jesus Christ encountered demon possessed men in Matthew 8:28-29, the demons cried out, *"What do you want with us, Son of God?" they shouted. "Have you come here to torture us **before the appointed time?**"* Another account of Jesus' encounter with a legion of demons is described in Luke 8:27-33, and in verse 31, the demons beg Jesus Christ not to send them into the abyss.

According to the above Scriptures, demons reasoned with Jesus Christ about torturing them before the appointed time. Also they begged Him not to cast them into the abyss. The Bible describes an appointed time for Satan and his demons to be cast into the abyss (the bottomless pit) in Revelation 20:1-3 and finally into the lake of fire in Revelation 20:10:

> *Then I saw an angel coming down from heaven, having the key to the bottomless pit and a great chain in his hand. He laid hold of **the dragon, that serpent of old, who is the Devil and Satan**, and bound him for a thousand years; and **he cast him into the bottomless pit, and shut him up**, and set a seal on him, so that he should deceive the nations no more till the thousand years were finished. But after these things he must be released for a little while.* (Revelation 20:1-3)

> **The devil, who deceived them, was cast into the lake of fire** *and brimstone where the beast and the false*

prophet are. And they will be tormented day and night forever and ever. (Revelation 20:10)

According to the above Scriptures, until the appointed day is fulfilled, Satan, principalities, powers, and the rulers of the darkness of this age cannot be bound or cast into the abyss or the lake of fire. What, then, are the followers of Jesus Christ authorized to do until the second coming of Christ? It is written in Matthew 10:7-8, *"And as you go, preach, saying, 'The kingdom of heaven is at hand.' Heal the sick, cleanse the lepers, raise the dead, cast out demons. Freely you have received, freely give."* Believers in Christ are authorized to 1) **preach** the kingdom of heaven; 2) **heal** the sick; 3) **cleanse** the lepers; 4) **raise** the dead; 5) **cast out** demons on the earth.

The followers of Jesus Christ are authorized to cast out earthbound demons—foot soldiers of the devil that are assigned to inflict targeted people with curses, sicknesses, bondages, additions, fear, depression, oppression, etc. However, believers of Christ are not authorized to bind or cast Satan, principalities, powers of the air and the rulers of darkness of this age and spiritual hosts of wickedness **in the heavenly places** (in the second heavenly realm) into the abyss before their appointed time. At the end, it will be an angel's job to cast Satan into the bottomless pit.

Not only that, believers in Christ must also take spiritual responsibility for their own lives. They must not solely depend on other believers to intercede for their own spiritual wellbeing. They need to declare the appropriate word of God over their lives by praying with the authority of Christ and the power of the Holy Spirit to route the wicked schemes of the power of darkness each day. If we believe in the victory that Jesus Christ won over Satan at the cross, we can be more than conquerors as we draw near to God by resisting every temptation of the devil.⁵

SATAN IS A MURDERER AND A LIAR

Jesus Christ declared who Satan is very clearly in John 8:44, *"He was a **murderer** from the beginning, and does not stand in the truth, because **there is no truth in him**. When he speaks a lie, he speaks from his own resources, for **he is a liar and the father of it**."* If Satan is a murderer and a liar, then believers in Christ must shun him at all cost and neither engage in dialoguing with him over any matters nor directly launch spiritual warfare against him. Jesus Christ never initiated communication with Satan nor did He try to bind him while He was walking on the earth.

It was Satan who initiated tempting Jesus to sin against the Father in Matthew 4:11. Jesus Christ refuted each of Satan's temptation by simply declaring, *"It is written"* with the appropriate Word of God until he left Him. Jesus Christ also warned His followers in John 10:10 about the schemes of the devil: *"The thief (the devil or false prophets) does not come except **to steal, and to kill [thuo: offer sacrifice], and to destroy**. I have come that they may have life, and that they may have it more abundantly."*

That means if anyone allows the devil to come into his life, then the devil has only one purpose for that person—to steal every blessing that God has given him and to kill God's divine creation mandate for him so he can be offered as a sacrifice to the devil. The ultimate goal is to destroy every aspect of God appointed divine life for him so Satan can take him into eternal hell with him. However, Jesus Christ declares that He has come to His chosen believers so that they may have life [*zoe*: self-existing life of God from heaven] and that they may have it more abundantly [*perissos*: excessive, superfluous, surplus]. That means the *zoe* will release God's love, joy, peace, abundant blessings, divine life, health, provision, and anointing to His children so they can do His work on earth for His glory each day. If we become one with Christ by being born-again in Him, we can enjoy the same abundant life that Adam and Eve enjoyed by being in God's divine glory and presence before they sinned.

The first Adam lost *zoe* (life of God) when he sinned against God, but the last Adam—Jesus Christ restored *zoe*—self-existing life of God, back to all who become sons and daughters of God by living inside of them. Because Jesus Christ lives inside of every believer with His divine life, we will never lose *zoe* again. God's *zoe* will release His abundant life on earth and eternal life in heaven to His sons and daughters. Therefore, the children of God with *zoe* from Christ residing inside of them can boldly declare, **"Your kingdom come and Your will be done on earth as it is in heaven."**

THE METHOD OF SATAN'S DECEPTION

The ultimate schemes of Satan for human beings are for them to believe his distortions, lies and manipulations against the truth of the word of God leading them to sin against His laws, statutes and commandments. As they fall into sinning before God, they become enslaved by the power of Satan to be his puppets to do all kinds of evil activities without ever experiencing God's *zoe*—abundant life in Christ. Therefore, the consequence of sin without repentance before God will be to bring His judgment upon themselves while on the earth and eventually to be cast into the lake of fire with Satan in the future. Let's examine three methods of Satan's deception:

- **Distortion**: It means to twist out of the true meaning. Satan distorted the true meaning of God's divine commandment to Adam and Eve in Genesis 3:1 by asking a distorted question, *"Has God indeed said, 'You shall not eat of every tree of the garden?'"* Satan usually launches his wicked dialogue with his intended victims to cause them to doubt the perfect will, plan, purpose, commandments and ways that have been established in the word of God.

  One of the devil's primary tools for launching an evil scheme in any person is to cause his deception to land into their heart by contradicting and distorting the truth. He already has a great tool to work with because of the Bible says, *"The heart is deceitful above all things, and desperately wicked: who can know it? (Jeremiah 17:9)"* You already have two strikes against you. Your heart seems to be ready to turn on you at any minute, and Satan is dedicated to seeing that it does just that! Sadly, most human hearts follow the deceiver more than God most of the time.[6]

  Once anyone has been engaged in a dialogue with Satan, one will be no match to the wicked craftiness of the deceiver. Therefore, we must quickly terminate any conversation with the devil in our flesh, soul, and spirit realms and draw ourselves near to the light of God by rendering spiritual prayers before Him. Then the light of God will swallow up the power of darkness in your mind and heart and set you free from Satan's wicked schemes.

- **Lies:** Once anyone has been enticed into Satan's tactics of distortion, he will directly lead them to believe in his lies. Even though Eve knew the commandment of God and answered Satan correctly in Genesis 3:2-3, *"We may eat the fruit of the trees of the garden; but of the fruit of the* tree which is in the midst of the garden, God has said, 'You shall not eat it, nor shall you touch it, lest you die'"; as she began to pay attention to Satan's enticing voice, he boldly lied and stated his own word absolutely against what the Lord had commanded in Genesis 3:4 by saying, *"You will not surely die."*

As Satan successfully dialogued with the woman with a distorted question and enticed her with his wicked scheme, he was able to launch his best tactic of lying into her mind with very crafty reasoning that caused her to seriously doubt the word of God in her heart. If anyone entertains Satan's reasoning thoughts in their heart, his evil power will entice them to disobey God and cause them to fall into his wicked trap and be enslaved to do his evil plans for their life. The consequence of that will be for Satan to come into their life to steal, kill and destroy God's wonderful plan for them.

- **Manipulation**: It means to control or plan upon by artful, unfair, or insidious means to one's own advantage. Once Satan's wicked schemes of distortion and lies infiltrated the woman's (Eve's) heart, he began to lead her into his deadliest plot. The serpent manipulated her mind to cause her to disobey God's commandment in Genesis 3:5, *"For God knows that in the day you eat of it your eyes will be opened, and you will be like God, knowing good and evil."*

Satan's manipulation of Eve was to convince her that God was intentionally blinding her spiritual eyes so that she would not experience the new scope of reality in the Garden of Eden. The next step was for Satan to make Eve believe that **she would be like God—knowing good and evil for herself.** Why was that the most deadly manipulation for Eve? Because Satan was manipulating her to believe that she wouldn't need to depend on God for everything anymore. The moment she disobeyed God's commandment by eating the forbidden fruit, her spiritual eyes would be opened and she would be like God—therefore she could be her own god and choose what would be good or evil for her by her own volition. Just as Satan wanted to be like God in heaven so he could choose to do what would be good or evil for himself without submitting to the Lord's guidance, he manipulated Adam and Eve to follow his wicked scheme to be their own gods on earth.

From the fall of man, the greatest struggle for any human beings have been either to choose to obey and follow God's ways or to follow their own understanding and plans for their own lives. Whenever any human beings have been standing on the juncture of two decisions, Satan would come and manipulate them to follow his wicked schemes against God. Therefore, when Satan comes to manipulate your choice of decisions, instead of entertaining his evil manipulative voice, you must resist his temptation and quickly draw near to God by praying and seeking His will for that matter. Then God's authority, power and wisdom will direct your heart and mind to follow His perfect ways for His glory.

THE PROCESS OF MAN'S FALL

Man lives in a body (flesh) that has a soul and a spirit. In order for Satan to control man's body and to get him to do his will, he must control man's will. The will is part of the soul of man. The soul is the mind, the emotions and the will of man. Satan will try to control our actions by deceiving us concerning the truth. One of Satan's most effective ways is to keep us ignorant of God's Word and to cause us to disobey His truth. If we do not know the truth, we will come into Satan's bondage.[7]

Satan always tempts us to fall into his wicked plans by slowly infiltrating into our physiological (fleshly) realm to entice our fleshly desires—such as the lust of the eyes and the flesh. Once we allow Satan's temptation into our fleshly sphere to entertain his wicked thoughts, he will gradually move into our psychological (soulish) domain to cause us to obey his evil schemes. As Satan's temptation penetrates our soulish area, next he goes into our deep spiritual realm to totally control us with his wicked power and making us powerless to obey God's will. At this stage, we can say that we have been demonized and become a slave to the devil's wicked schemes.

Let's examine how Eve fell into the above process and sinned against God's commandment in Genesis 3:6:

- **Temptation in physiological (fleshly) area**: *"So when the woman saw that the tree was good for food..."* Eve had seen the tree and its fruit many times but never had a desire to either touch it or to eat of its fruit prior to Satan's temptation. However, as she began paying attention to his enticing voice about eating the forbidden fruit in her fleshly realm, the lust of her eyes and her flesh was planted in her heart.

  After the temptation entered into her flesh, she began to look at the fruit with lustful eyes—*"the tree was good for food..."* Even though Eve was enticed to look at the fruit with lustful eyes, if she had changed her mind and decided not to sin, then she might not have sinned against God's commandment. Just being tempted in one's eyes in and of itself is not a sin; however, yielding to the temptation and taking action is to commit sin against God.

- **Temptation in psychological (soulish) realm:** *"It was pleasant to the eyes."* At first, Eve was only thinking about the fruit being good for food to satisfy her fleshly desire. But Satan was enticing her into thinking about that it was pleasant to the soulish eyes—he was causing his temptation to sink into her soul so she would be coming one step closer to committing sin against God. The flesh of a human being desires only to satisfy its basic needs, such senses as seeing, smelling, touching, hearing, and tasting.

  However, the soul desires to feel and experience the matters that satisfy the emotional needs such as feeling loved, accepted, recognized, experimented, excited, needed, filled with joy, satisfied to the eyes of the soul, etc. Once anyone invites Satan's temptation into one's soul domain, one is one step closer to committing sin by acting it out in one's fleshly realms. This is because the flesh has a natural tendency of becoming a slave to the soul's desire.

  If one's soul is happy, then the flesh will smile and express the happiness. But when one's soul is sad and depressed, then the flesh will manifest sadness and depression in action. Therefore, Satan's great desire is to entice the soul to agree with his wicked evil plans. Once the soul surrenders to Satan's temptation, the person will normally carry out his evil plan in action—such as abusing alcohol and drugs, sexual addictions and many other bondages that are described in 1 Corinthians 6:9-10:

  > *Do you not know that the unrighteous will not inherit the kingdom of God? Do not be deceived.*

Neither fornicators, nor idolaters, nor adulterers, nor homosexuals, nor sodomites, nor thieves, nor covetous, nor drunkards, nor revilers, nor extortioners will inherit the kingdom of God.

- **Temptation in spiritual area:** *"A tree desirable to make one wise, she took of its fruit and ate. She also gave to her husband with her, and he ate."* In this stage of temptation, Eve allowed Satan's evil scheme to enter into its final stage—her spiritual realm. Once anyone invites Satan's wicked plan to enter into the spiritual domain, now one's fate has been sealed and one will be bound by his wicked evil purpose.

As Eve entertained the thought that the forbidden tree was desirable because it would make her wise in her spirit, she invited Satan's final scheme to control her fleshly, soulish and spiritual realms and she fell—Eve took of the fruit and ate, and gave it to Adam and he ate. Both of them fell from the glory of God and began to hide themselves from the presence of God in Genesis 3:9-13:

> *Then the Lord God called to Adam and said to him, '**Where are you?**' So he said, 'I heard Your voice in the garden, and I was afraid **because I was naked; and I hid myself.**' And He said, 'Who told you that you were naked? **Have you eaten from the tree of which I commanded you that you should not eat?**' Then the man said, 'The woman whom You gave to be with me, she gave me of the tree, and I ate.' And the Lord God said to the woman, 'What is this you have done?' The woman said, '**The serpent deceived me, and I ate.**'*

The saddest reality and reaction of fallen Adam and Eve after committing sin before the Lord was that **they began to hide themselves from the presence of God** (Genesis 3:8-9). The final consequence of their action caused them to lose the very intimate communion with the Creator God as their Father, Lord, Savior, Provider, Life, Sustainer, Joy, Peace, Lover, Protector, etc. They became their own gods to rule their lives according to their own desires to choose good and evil for themselves.

Adam and Eve were cast out of the Garden of Eden (the paradise on the earth) and their descendants inherited the earth that had been infested by the curses that God pronounced in Genesis 3:14-19. The Devil will always cause any fallen human beings to be tempted in their fleshly area first; after penetrating into the physiological realm, then he will proceed to entice their soulish area for them to be bound by his evil schemes; and finally, he will invade their spiritual domain to paralyze them to do his wicked evil plans for their lives.

However, when the Lord through the Holy Spirit regenerates any fallen human beings to be saved, He first deals with their spirit so that they may yield to the convicting voice of the Holy Spirit. Once they invite the Holy Spirit to enter into their spirit to be resurrected from the bondages of their sinful life style, then He will guide them to repent of all the sins they have committed in their soulish area. As the regenerating Holy Spirit's conviction enters into the soulish realm, they will be ready to turn away from their wicked ways and this will cause their fleshly domain to submit to the call of the Spirit for salvation.

Finally, a person yields one's spirit, soul and flesh to the Lord Jesus Christ by repenting of all one's sins, then one will be born again in Christ and become a new creation in Him. Therefore, God will always regenerate any fallen human being by entering into one's spirit first, then secondly, He will deal with one's soulish area, and lastly, He will help one to overcome one's fleshly realm so one can be set free from the bondages of Satan and become a son or a daughter of God. Therefore John 8:36 states, *"If the Son makes you free, you shall be free indeed."* Also 2 Corinthians 3:17 states, *"Now the Lord is the Spirit; and where the Spirit of the Lord is, there is liberty."*

SATAN'S SCHEMES AGAINST HUMAN BEINGS

Since the fall of man, all of Adam's descendants have fallen short of the glory of God and been living under the curses and sin that infested the world by the devil. Multitudes of fallen souls all over the earth cry out each day, *"Oh How I want to break free from the bondages of sin in my life."* Some of the curses that fallen human beings have been in bondage to are rebellion, idolatry, witchcraft, jealousy, lies, anger, deception, sexual immorality, manipulations, unforgiveness, addiction, hatred, covetousness, drunkenness, condemnation, judgment, critical spirit, fear, prejudice, religious spirits, pride, etc.

The following Scriptures confirm the condition of fallen mankind and their ultimate destiny:

> **Do you not know that the unrighteous will not inherit the kingdom of God?** *Do not be deceived. Neither fornicators, nor idolaters, nor adulterers, nor homosexuals, nor sodomites, nor thieves, nor covetous, nor drunkards, nor revilers, nor extortioners will inherit the kingdom of God.* (1 Corinthians 6:9-10)

*Now the works of the flesh are evident, which are: adultery, fornication, uncleanness, lewdness, idolatry, sorcery, hatred, contentions, jealousies, outbursts of wrath, selfish ambitions, dissensions, heresies, envy, murders, drunkenness, revelries, and the like; of which I tell you beforehand, just as I also told you in time past, that **those who practice such things will not inherit the kingdom of God.*** (Galatians 5:19-21)

Satan will see that his sinful pleasures satisfy you until his claws have burrowed deep into your soul. He will kiss you on the cheek and whisper empty promises into your love-struck ear. He will use his dazzling array of sinful pleasures to woo you into his bedchamber, lull you to sleep, and then use and abuse you and stab you in the back! He will promise you everything and leave you with nothing. His favorite lie is to promise you heaven on earth, but will give you eternity in hell. He is more than willing to love you for a season so he can curse you for eternity.[8]

Therefore, we must repent of our sinful lifestyle and accept Jesus Christ as our Lord and Savior so we can inherit the kingdom of God according to His promises in John 3:16, Romans 10:9-10, and Romans 6:23:

*For God so loved the world that He gave His only begotten Son, that **whoever believes in Him should not perish but have everlasting life.*** (John 3:16)

If you confess with your mouth the Lord Jesus and believe in your heart that God has raised Him from the dead, you will be saved. *For with the heart one believes unto righteousness, and with the mouth confession is made unto salvation.* (Romans 10:9-10)

For the wages of sin is death, but the gift of God is eternal life in Christ Jesus our Lord. (Romans 6:23)

One of the deadliest poisons Satan had injected for human beings to taste was the lies that he spoke to Eve in Genesis 3:4-5:

*Then the serpent said to the woman, 'You will not surely die. For God knows that in the day you eat of it your eyes will be opened, and **you will be like God, knowing good and evil**.*

According to the above Scriptures, Satan was suggesting to Adam and Eve that they would not surely die even though they would be disobeying God's one command in the Garden of Eden. Not only that their spiritual eyes would be opened to be like God so they wouldn't need to depend on His presence, power, wisdom, and guidance anymore, but also they could be like God and choose to know good and evil for themselves by relying on their own understanding.

The fruit of the above thinking has been manifesting in our post-modern Christian world in the Western countries. What seems most significant is the fact that only a few years ago Christians would have gotten up and walked out on anyone who tried to suggest to them that they are gods. That no longer seems to be the case in the United States of America. Today many Christians influenced by the New Age belief system, believe not that they are going to become gods like the Mormons but that they already are gods, like the Hindus, and just need to "realize" it. And they support this idea with selected Bible verses: Jesus Christ asked the Pharisees this question in John 10:34, "*Is it not written in your law that I said, 'You are gods?'*"

The Bible never says that God made man a god, or that He promised man that he could become a god. That was Satan's seductive promise to Eve, and it brought the knowledge of good and evil, and that knowledge (forbidden by God) destroyed the man and woman whom God had made. They had become "gods," "knowing good and evil."[9] Therefore, we must repent of our sins of trying to become gods so we can decide good and evil for ourselves. But we should accept the gift of God, Jesus Christ, and be truly saved and totally rely on His wisdom, authority and power to guide our lives according to His perfect will.

SATAN'S INFLUENCE ON THE CHURCH

Although Satan knew he was defeated, he would not go down without a fight. He lost the war in the third heavenly realm and was cast into the earth. Now his focus is to defeat God's plan for His chosen disciples on earth. His evil plan of attack: he would take as many people down to the lake of fire as he could, and he would do everything possible to neutralize his enemy—the Church of the living God. Satan has been deceiving, manipulating and binding God's people to fall into the same fate that he had inherited through rebellion, disobedience and lawlessness. Therefore, Satan is doing whatever he can to render Christians powerless and impotent by enticing them to be disobedient to the Word of God.[10]

Satan hates the activities of God's children which expand His kingdom on earth and fulfill His prophecy in Matthew 24:14, *"And this gospel of the kingdom will be preached in all the world as a witness to all the nations* [ethne: every people group]*, and then the end will come."* When every Unreached People Group hears the gospel of the kingdom of God, then the end will come—Jesus Christ will come back to rule the earth for a thousand years (Revelation 20:4) and Satan will be bound and cast into the bottomless pit (Revelation 20:1-3). In order for Matthew 24:14 to be fulfilled, prior to Christ's ascension to heaven, Jesus gave His disciples the Great Commission in Matthew 28:18-20 and Acts 1:8:

> *All authority has been given to Me in heaven and on earth.* ***Go therefore and make disciples of all the nations****, baptizing them in the name of the Father and of the Son and of the Holy Spirit, teaching them to observe all things that I have commanded you; and lo, I am with you always, even to the end of the age.*
> (Revelation 28:18-20)

> *But you shall receive power when the Holy Spirit has come upon you;* ***and you shall be witnesses to Me in Jerusalem, and in all Judea and Samaria, and to the end of the earth****.* (Acts 1:8)

After Jesus Christ gave His disciples the Great Commission, He commanded them to wait on the Promise of the Father—the Holy Spirit to come down upon them and empower them to fulfill the call in Acts 1:8. On the day of Pentecost, the power of the Holy Spirit came down upon 120 believers that were praying in the upper room in Jerusalem (Acts 1:4-5, 13-15) and they were all filled with the Holy Spirit (Acts 2:1-4).

Once they were baptized with the Holy Spirit, God knew that they needed the body of Christ (church) to be engaged in expanding the kingdom of God from Jerusalem to the end of the earth. Therefore, the Holy Spirit established the first Jerusalem church to initiate His worldwide missions to fulfill the Great Commission. Therefore, Satan began to persecute the Church so that he could have more time on earth to hinder, by every possible means, the Church of the living God from engaging in fulfilling the prophecy in Matthew 24:14. The following are some of the tactics of Satan that have been used against God's Church in the world:

- **The loveless church** (Revelation 2:1-7): Satan's desire for any church is to cause it to lose its first love—evangelizing its own Jerusalem to the end of the earth. When a church loses its first love, it will become a very well organized religious and social gathering place where the Spirit of the Lord has ceased to move. Their programs and religious performances in the name of God will entertain the church members without ever witnessing the book of Acts revival with signs, wonders and miracles following. Thus, Jesus Christ warned the church of Ephesus in Revelation 2:2-5:

    I know your works, your labor, your patience, and that you cannot bear those who are evil. And you have tested those who say they are apostles and are not, and have found them liars; and you have persevered and have patience, and have labored for My name's sake and have not become weary. ***Nevertheless I have this against you, that you have left your first love.*** *Remember therefore from where you have fallen; repent and do the first works, or else **I will come to you quickly and remove your lampstand from its place—unless you repent.***

    As I traveled to more than 100 countries in the world, I have witnessed multitudes of small, medium and large churches that have lost their lampstands (anointing of the Holy Spirit) and replaced the presence of God with many programs and performances of religious activities. It is the subtle work of Satan that causes the Church of the living God to lose its first love and power to be Christ's witness among their own communities and in the nations.

- **The corrupt church** (Revelation 2:18-29): Another tactic of Satan is to corrupt the leadership of a church by releasing the spirit of Jezebel which causes them to engage in sexual immorality and many other forms of abominable activities such as idol worship, false teachings, mismanagement of finances, etc. Even though a church has been totally influenced by the spirit of Jezebel, it may appear to be a well-functioning body prior to the sin being exposed as described in Revelation 2:19:

> *I know your works,* ***love, service, faith, and your patience****; and as for your works, the last are more than the first.*

When we examine the above Scripture, the church in Thyatira appears to be a very well functioning church demonstrating good works, having love among the members and various kinds of services to minister to the body with faith and patience in God. However, Jesus Christ, who knew what was really going on in the leadership of the church, spoke the following words in Revelation 2:20-22:

> *Nevertheless I have a few things against you, because* ***you allow that woman Jezebel, who calls herself a prophetess, to teach and seduce My servants to commit sexual immorality and eat things sacrificed to idols****. And I gave her **time to repent** of her sexual immorality, and she did not repent. Indeed I will cast her into a sickbed, and*

*those who commit adultery with her into great tribulation, **unless they repent of their deeds**.*

When Satan sends a woman who is bound by the spirit of Jezebel to corrupt the church, she will initially do everything possible to serve the leadership of the church, especially the senior pastor with her great commitment and devotion. She will begin to demonstrate her prophetic gifts that are from Satan to cause the senior leaders to believe that she is a very committed, dedicated and a spiritual asset to the church. She will gradually rise to be a very close spiritual and mental assistant to the senior leader until she seduces him to fall into sexual sin with her.

Once she engages in sexual sin with the senior leader, she begins to control the church with Satan's wicked plans and cause it to become a very corrupted church. However, even though the woman Jezebel caused such an abominable sin by the leadership of the church, Jesus Christ gave her time to repent of her sexual immorality, but she did not repent. How merciful God is! True repentance can bring God's healing to even to a corrupt church.

- **The lukewarm church** (Revelation 3:14-22): Satan doesn't want any of God's churches to be on fire for Him and His callings, but to be lukewarm religious and social gathering places without the power of the Holy Spirit moving in action. As long as a church becomes a lukewarm religious place, it is no real threat to the kingdom of darkness on the earth. Therefore, Jesus Christ spoke to the church of the Laodiceans about the condition of the lukewarm church:

> *I know your works, that you are neither cold nor hot. I could wish you were cold or hot. So then, because you are lukewarm, and neither cold nor hot, I will vomit you out of My mouth.*
> (Revelation 3:15-16)

Obviously, a lukewarm church will be vomited out of the mouth of Jesus Christ because it is not useful for the works of the kingdom of God on the earth. A lukewarm church is a people oriented church that is more concerned about following the dead traditions and religious orders than what the Holy Spirit wants to do with the church. Every activity and message of the church is all about behavior modification and politically correct teachings that try to appease and satisfy all different types of people in the congregation. Their approach to Christianity is to simply provide a safe place for the members and not ever addressing the message of the cross of Jesus Christ that requires the followers to truly repent from their sinful lifestyles. Thus, Jesus Christ describes the conditions of the lukewarm church in Revelation 3:17-18:

> *Because you say, '**I am rich, have become wealthy, and have need of nothing**'—and do not know that you are **wretched, miserable, poor, blind, and naked**—I counsel you to buy from Me gold refined in the fire, that you may be rich; and white garments, that you may be clothed, that **the shame of your nakedness may not be revealed**; and anoint your eyes with eye salve, that you may see.*

The above Scriptures clearly describe the conditions of many wealthy churches in economically advanced countries. They believe that they are wealthy and have need of nothing in their outwardly appearances before God and men; however, Jesus Christ considers them spiritually wretched, miserable, poor, blind, and naked and shameless of their nakedness. The fire of the Holy Spirit died out a long time ago and they don't even know that Jesus Christ has shunned the church. Therefore, Jesus Christ is calling the lukewarm church to repent so that He can come in and turn it into the inflamed body of Christ it once was by the power of the Holy Spirit as He describes in Revelation 2:20:

> *Behold, I stand at the door and knock.* ***If anyone hears My voice and opens the door, I will come in*** *to him (the lukewarm church) and dine with him, and he with Me.*

- **The compromising church** (Revelation 2:12-17): Satan would love to cause God's anointed church to become a compromising church so that the power and presence of God could be replaced by the programs and performing activities that serve to help it gain more members so it can maintain its status quo. They will only choose selected Scriptures that justify their compromising stands on social issues such as abortion, homosexuality and LGBTQ agenda, political parties, etc. Therefore, Jesus Christ spoke to the church of Pergamos in Revelation 2:13:

> *I know your works, and where you dwell,* ***where Satan's throne is****. And you hold fast to My name, and did not deny My faith...*

According to the above Scripture, it appears that the church was located in a city in which Satan's throne was and he had very strong influence in the city with his wicked plans. However, Jesus Christ commended them for holding fast to His name and not denying His faith (perhaps in outwardly appearance only). Nevertheless, in the following Scriptures, Jesus rebuked them for their serious involvement in compromising the teachings of the church in Revelation 2:14-15:

> *But I have a few things against you, because you have there those who hold **the doctrine of Balaam**, who taught Balak to put a stumbling block before the children of Israel, to eat things sacrificed to idols, and to commit sexual immorality. Thus you also have those who hold **the doctrine of the Nicolaitans**, which thing I hate.*

What is the doctrine of Balaam? The original stories of Balaam are written in Numbers 22-25. Balak, the king of the Moabites, promised to greatly reward Balaam, a supposed prophet of God, if he would curse the Israelites (Numbers 22:16-17). However, God said to Balaam in Numbers 22:12, *"You shall not go with them; you shall not curse the people, for they are blessed."* Even though he knew the perfect will of God, Balaam refused to obey Him and continuously followed Balak's direction to curse the Israelites. God, however, put His words in Balaam's mouth and blessed the Israelites rather than cursing them each time. In verse 11 of Jude, the Scripture states, *"Like Balaam, they deceive people for money* (NLT)." Also *"the way of Balaam"* is described in 2 Peter 2:12, 15-16 (NLT):

> *These false teachers are like unthinking animals, creatures of instinct, born to be caught and*

*destroyed. They scoff at things they do not understand, and like animals, they will be destroyed...They have wandered off the right road and followed **the footsteps of Balaam son of Beor, who loved to earn money by doing wrong.** But Balaam was stopped from his mad course when his donkey rebuked him with a human voice.*

Therefore, the way of Balaam describes unrighteous pastors, prophets, and ministers of the gospel who build their own kingdoms on earth by gaining wealth by every possible means including teaching many false doctrines in the name of God.

What is the doctrine of the Nicolaitans? The word *"Nicolaitans"* means, *"to be victorious over the people,"* or *"to conquer the people."* Therefore, it might have meant that the senior leaders of a church or ministry control the rest of the congregation with their total authoritarian style of leadership. They have forgotten the true meaning of biblical leadership, which is to serve God's people by being led by the guidance of the Holy Spirit as good shepherds. Unfortunately, they follow the same examples of worldly corporate models—such titles as the CEO of a church, Executive Pastor, CFO of the ministry, etc. God hates the practice and doctrine of the Nicolaitans according to Revelation 2:15.

- **The dead Church** (Revelation 3:1-6): Satan would love to cause the Church to have the name of being alive, but in reality, it is spiritually dead. How can Satan make a living church to become a spiritually dead one? I believe that the answer is written in 2 Timothy 3:1-5:

> *But know this, that in the last days perilous times will come: For men will be lovers of themselves, lovers of money, boasters, proud, blasphemers, disobedient to parents, unthankful, unholy, unloving, unforgiving, slanderers, without self-control, brutal, despisers of good, traitors, headstrong, haughty, lovers of pleasure rather than lovers of God, **having a form of godliness but denying its power**. And from such people turn away!*

When a church is not preaching Jesus Christ and Him crucified, but only teaching motivational messages without demonstrating His kingdom authority and power, then it can easily become a church having a form of godliness but denying its power. It will become a dead church without the move of the Holy Spirit. Therefore, Jesus Christ spoke to the church in Sardis in Revelation 3:1-3:

> *I know your works, that **you have a name that you are alive, but you are dead**. Be watchful, and strengthen the things which remain, that are ready to die, for I have not found your works perfect before God. Remember therefore how you have received and heard; **hold fast and repent**. Therefore if you will not watch, I will come upon you as a thief, and you will not know what hour I will come upon you.*

I believe that nearly all church leaders and mature believers across our country today would agree that we urgently need a genuine spiritual revival. Part of our problem is that we have developed a religious industry whose machinery runs smoothly without any need of the Holy Spirit—thus creating dead churches. We created a people oriented, program based, and religious churches that haven't experienced the presence of God for a long time. A. W. Tozer once commented that if God were to take the Holy Spirit out of this world, most of what the church is doing would go right on, and nobody would know the difference. We have established the Church according to our ways and control systems—but they are not operating in the ways of the Holy Spirit to release God's presence, healing, deliverance, and power.

The churches in Acts had no New Testament Bible (It had yet to be written), no choirs, no electronic equipment, no buildings of their own, no hierarchical leadership positions except the fivefold ministries—and yet they still shook the world with the power of the Holy Spirit. God didn't send the Holy Spirit to give us thrills and chills; he sent the Spirit to empower us to win lost souls to Christ and to destroy the works of the devil by signs, wonders, and miracles following.

The root problem is the need for the Holy Spirit to come in power and birth a true spirit of prayer and revival. In other words, we must first secure the Spirit's presence and grace; then we can move out in powerful praying for all kinds of other needs by fulfilling the command of Christ in Matthew 10:7-8.[11]

There are too many churches that have names under different denominational affiliations, but in the eyes of God they are spiritually dead—they have forms of godliness but are denying the power of God. Satan wants God's churches to be dead, powerless and impotent religious entities without having the power of the Holy Spirit causing the River of Life to flow freely. The Apostle Paul wrote about witchcraft's effect on born-again, Spirit-filled believers—people who had tasted, seen, and experienced the miraculous power of God in Galatians 3:1-5. The believers in Galatia received the gift of the Holy Spirit and witnessed the working of miracles, and yet Paul says that they were bewitched!

Did you know that a church could be filled with good, Spirit-filled people, and yet be oblivious to a move of God in their midst? They can hear an anointed word from the heart of God, but remain unable to respond—almost as if a spell had been cast on them. Many modern-day churches have one thing in common with the church in Galatia—bewitchment which has obscured the cross and the power of the Holy Spirit.[12]

- **The persecuted church** (Revelation 2:8-11): When a church is alive in the authority of Jesus Christ and the power of the Holy Spirit, then Satan will do everything possible to cause the fire of God to die down or to raise severe persecution to dismantle the church. Unfortunately, the persecution will come from the government, social and religious orders, and other bodies of Christ against the church, which is filled with the presence of the Holy Spirit and power. Thus, Jesus Christ spoke to the church in Smyrna in Revelation 2:9-10:

  > *I know your works,* ***tribulation, and poverty (but you are rich)****; and I know the blasphemy of those who say they are Jews and are not, but are a synagogue of Satan.* ***Do not fear any of those things which you are about to suffer.*** *Indeed, the devil is about to throw some of you into prison, that you may be tested, and you will have tribulation ten days.* ***Be faithful until death, and I will give you the crown of life.***

Jesus Christ declared that He knew their works, tribulation and physical poverty (but they were spiritually rich). He encouraged them not to fear any of the persecutions they were about to suffer and charged them to be faithful even unto death so they could receive the crown of life. At times, God will not rescue us from going through various forms of persecution in this world; however, He will go through them with us and strengthen us to be faithful even unto death.

The underground house church leaders in Asia have been terribly persecuted by the government for many decades. I met one leader who had been in jail for over 16 years. He shared with me about numerous tortures, beatings, brain washing interrogations, and hard labor he had to endure. One time, four prison guards came into his jail cell and told him to take off all his clothes. It was a very cold winter night, approximately minus 20 degrees Fahrenheit outside. They cut off all the heat sources in his room and they tied each of his hands and legs with four ropes.

They pulled the ropes so hard his body was suspended in air. They tied the four ropes to four hooks on the walls and left him to freeze to death. He told me that he was in agonizing pain so he prayed to the Lord to take him to heaven quickly because he couldn't endure any longer. Within 10 minutes, his whole body began to freeze so he closed his eyes and asked the Lord to receive him into the kingdom of heaven. Suddenly, he saw two big angels with two enormous wings on their backs come into the jail cell. One of them told him that he would not die that night but assured him that he would be released from the prison the following morning. Then they covered his frozen body with their wings. He told me that he began to feel so warm that he went into a deep sleep without feeling any more pain in his arms and legs. The next morning, the same four jail guards came into his cell to take away his dead frozen body.

However, when they came in, they discovered that he was sweating so much that he had a puddle of sweat underneath his body. They were shocked about the fact that he was not only alive but was also sweating with steam rising from his body. They untied him and released him that very afternoon from the prison. He was even faithful unto death but God rescued him to serve Him in a hostile and persecuted land. He is still serving the Lord as one of the leaders in the underground house churches. We, the disciples of Christ, must endure hardships, tribulations and persecutions as His chosen soldiers.

- **The faithful church** (Revelation 3:7-13): It is wonderful to know that there is and will always be faithful churches in the eyes of Jesus Christ regardless of the many churches that have fallen away from Him. Therefore, He spoke to the church in Philadelphia in Revelation 3:7-8, 10-12:

  *He who has the key of David, He who opens and no one shuts, and shuts and no one opens": "I know your works. See, I have **set before you an open door, and no one can shut it**; for you have a little strength, have kept My word, and have not denied My name." Because **you have kept My command to persevere, I also will keep you from the hour of trial** which shall come upon the whole world, to test those who dwell on the earth. Behold, I am coming quickly! Hold fast what you have, that no one may take your crown. He who overcomes, I will make him a pillar in the temple of My God, and he* *shall go out no more. I will write on him the name of My God and the name of the city of My God, the New Jerusalem, which comes down out of heaven from My God. And I will write on him My new name.*

Jesus Christ assures the faithful church, "*I have set before you an open door, and no one can shut it, because you have kept My command to persevere, I also will keep you from the hour of trial.*" We, the disciples of Christ, are the Church of the living God and we must be very faithful to His commandments and obey His call to evangelize from our own Jerusalem to the ends of the earth. As we do that, Jesus Christ will set before us an open door of blessings, provisions, anointing, power and authority to accomplish the will of God in our lives.

We must not be conformed to this world and present our bodies as a living sacrifice unto to the Lord to be His faithful church:

I beseech you therefore, brethren, by the mercies of God, that you present your bodies a living sacrifice, holy, acceptable to God, which is your reasonable service. And ***do not be conformed to this world, but be transformed by the renewing of your mind****, that you may prove what is that good and acceptable and perfect will of God.*
(Romans 12:1-2)

Chapter 4

DEALING WITH SATAN IN THE OLD TESTAMENT

The heroes of the Old Testament never engaged in launching any spiritual warfare directly against Satan, but they totally depended on the mighty God to defeat his wicked evil schemes. Therefore, it is important for us to examine the Scriptures and learn the principles of how God's mighty men handled their struggles in dealing with Satan's assaults and temptations in the Old Testament era. **The Bible is the best "Spiritual Warfare" manual** for teaching God's children how to be correctly engaged in overcoming the power of darkness, far better than any of the spiritual warfare books written by men. This is because the stories of the heroes in the Bible always point us to focus on God's mighty presence and power to defeat the enemy. They never emphasize Satan's wicked power directly or indirectly.

THE STORY OF JOB

The Book of Job is considered to be the earliest written book in the Bible by many theological scholars. The book begins with a dialogue between God and Satan followed by three cycles of human debates between Job and his friends. Through God's permission, Satan launched his direct assault against Job, his possessions, livestock, servants, children and health. Job was a righteous man in his generation and he struggled with the question—Why have all these calamities come against him without any cause?

It concludes with God's divine encounter with Job describing his shortfalls. In the end, as Job acknowledged the sovereignty of God in his life and prayed for his friends, God blessed his latter days more than his former days. One thing is very clear in the book of Job: even though Satan directly assaulted Job, he never directly addressed the devil but only poured out his questions, complains and doubts before God. Now let's examine Job 1:6-12:

> *Now there was a day when the sons of God came to present themselves before the Lord, and **Satan also came among them**. And the Lord said to Satan, "From where do you come?" So Satan answered the Lord and said, "**From going to and fro on the earth, and from walking back and forth on it**." Then the Lord said to Satan, "**Have you considered My servant Job, that there is none like him on the earth, a blameless and upright man, one who fears God and shuns evil**?*
>
> *So Satan answered the Lord and said, "Does Job fear God for nothing? Have You not made a hedge around him, around his household, and around all that he has on every side? You have blessed the work of his hands, and his possessions have increased in the land. **But now, stretch out Your hand and touch all that he has, and he will surely curse You to Your face**!" And the Lord said to Satan, "Behold, all that he has is in your power; only do not lay a hand on his*

person." So Satan went out from the presence of the Lord.

According to the above Scriptures, Satan was able to come up and present himself to God in heaven in those days. However, Satan was already earthbound based on his answer in Job 1:7, *"From going to and fro on the earth, and from walking back and forth on it."* Then, God challenged Satan to consider Job whose reputation was *a blameless and upright man, one who fears God and shuns evil.* Insolent Satan responded by saying that God had put His special hedge of protection around all Job had. Thus, Satan dared to challenge God by saying if He would take away His coverings upon Job's life and touch his possessions, then he would curse God to His face. So God gave permission to Satan to touch all Job had. The assault of Satan against everything Job possessed began to take place in Job 1:13-22:

1) Job's possessions were destroyed (vss. 13-15)
2) Job's livestock was destroyed (vss. 16-17)
3) Job's servants were destroyed (vss. 16-17)
4) Job's 10 children were killed (vss. 18-19)
5) Job's health was touched (Job 2:7)

The above examples are very typical of how Satan attacks God's children with his evil and wicked tactics. However, I believe that God has to grant His permission for Satan to afflict His children. Then, you may ask, why would God give Satan His approval to torment His children? When God allows Satan to inflict his wicked attacks on His children, the outcome will always turn out to be for His glory if they will totally trust Him with their lives. God can turn what Satan meant for evil around for His own glory and victory for His children.

Also, God can use Satan to test one's heart to see what the response to his assault will be. Will the afflicted one humble oneself and turn to the Lord with a repentant heart and totally rely on Him for deliverance? Or will one blame Satan and begin to launch direct spiritual warfare against him? Or will one blame God and complain about everything that goes wrong in one's life? God might want to demonstrate His divine plan, purpose, and power for His chosen people through allowing Satan's wicked schemes to be launched against them.

What the devil meant for evil for His children, God can turn it around for His glory and equip them to be strong and courageous in the Lord. Therefore, we must praise the Lord even more when the enemy throws his many wicked temptations and assaults at us to destroy us. As we praise the Lord in the midst of Satan's attacks, we are truly demonstrating that we absolutely trust and depend on Him as our Deliverer and He will fight the battle for us.

JOB'S RESPONSE AFTER THE ASSAULT

Job didn't try to bind Satan or attempt to launch his spiritual warfare against the power of darkness in his own accord, but Job responded to God with his integrity, the fear of the Lord in his heart and absolute surrender to His divine will in Job 1:20-22:

> *Then Job arose, tore his robe, and shaved his head; and **he fell to the ground and worshiped**. And he said: 'Naked I came from my mother's womb, and naked shall I return there. The Lord gave, and the Lord has taken away; **blessed be the name of the Lord.**' In all this **Job did not sin nor charge God with wrong.**'*

We can identify why God considered Job to be a blameless, upright man, one who feared God and shunned evil in Job 1:8. Let's examine Job's initial three responses to Satan's attacks on him, his children, servants, possessions and his health:

1) **Job fell to the ground and worshiped the Lord**: When things are going well for anyone, it is very easy to praise the Lord and worship Him for all the good things that He has done. However, worshipping and praising the Lord when things are going terribly wrong is not easy for anyone to do. Satan wants us to be in despair, filled with sorrow, confused, downcast, fearful, defeated, blaming God, and charging after the devil, when we are afflicted and assaulted by him.

    Ultimately, Satan wants the one who has been afflicted by him to be so depressed and utterly destroyed that one will curse God and walk away from Him and His divine plan for one's life. Regardless of the situations and circumstances, God wants His children to be upright in heart and be glad in Him in Psalm 32:11, *"Be glad in the Lord and rejoice, you righteous; and shout for joy, all you upright in heart!"* Therefore, when things are going terribly wrong in life, it is the time to render unto the Lord a sacrifice of praise according to Philippians 4:4-7:

    > ***Rejoice in the Lord always.*** *Again I will say, rejoice! Let your gentleness be known to all men. The Lord is at hand.* ***Be anxious for nothing, but in everything by prayer and supplication****, with thanksgiving, let your requests be made known to God; and* ***the peace of God, which surpasses all under-***

standing, will guard your hearts and minds through Christ Jesus.

Can you imagine the sorrow that Job felt after losing all his 10 children in one day? Yet he chose to worship the Lord immediately after the terrible disaster. When one chooses to praise the Lord regardless of what terrible things have happened to him, then Satan loses his power over that person's life because God will be with him while he is going through the fiery trial.

2) **Job blessed the name of the Lord:** Regardless of Job's deep distress, he acknowledged the fact that the Lord had given him all he ever owned and it would be His prerogative to take it away from him. Once Job demonstrated his true heart before God even in his terrible losses, Satan began to lose his grip on his life.

Job not only worshiped the Lord but he also blessed the name of the Lord instead of fulfilling his wife's and Satan's desire in Job 2:9, *"Then his wife said to him, 'Do you still hold fast to your integrity? Curse God and die!'"* A righteous man, Job rebuked his wife by responding to her in Job 1:10, *"You speak as one of the foolish women speaks. Shall we indeed accept good from God, and shall we not accept adversity? In all this Job did not sin with his lips."*

3) **Job did not sin nor charge God with wrong:** We can truly learn from how Job responded to God when we face adversities that may have been launched by the devil. No matter what difficult situations may happen in life, we must never sin or charge God with wrong. God may allow certain things to happen to His

children, but He is the great, faithful, kind and loving Father and He will eventually turn them around for good for His own glory if we trust Him at all cost. As I have traveled to the nations and ministered to multitudes of people, I have encountered numerous Christians who blamed God for their misfortunes.

Some of them totally walked away from God because they were accusing Him of allowing the calamity to happen to them. Some could not understand how a loving God could allow such tragedy to occur to their believing family members. Others walked away just because God didn't answer their prayers the way they wanted.

I met a lady in Bulgaria whose 17-year-old daughter was killed in a car accident on the way to church. The mother was taking her daughter to the church to lead the worship team that morning but they were late so she insisted the taxi driver go faster. Driving over the speed limit, the driver ran a red light and collided with an oncoming truck. The driver and her daughter were killed but she survived.

Of course, it was a very tragic incident for the mother. She mourned for her daughter and also blamed herself for the accident. She would cry out to God saying, *"Why didn't you take me instead of my 17 year old daughter who had a full life ahead of her? How could you allow the accident to happen to us if you truly loved us, when we only wanted to go to the church to worship You?"*

The mother became very depressed and stopped going to the church. She didn't take care of her husband or her two younger living son and daughter for two years. Finally, her husband and two children came to her and told her that she loved her dead daughter more than them. Eventually, her husband divorced her and custody of two children was granted to him. On the day that her divorce was finalized, she lost all her hope and she was walking back to her lonely apartment to commit suicide. While she was crying and walking toward her apartment to die, she passed by the tent where I was ministering that night.

I was preaching about the message of life in Christ according to John 10:10, *"The thief does not come except to steal, and to kill, and to destroy. I have come that they may have life, and that they have it more abundantly."* As I was preaching that Satan would only come to steal, and to kill, and to destroy everything that belonged to God's children, she felt a strong hand pushing her into the tent. So she came into the tent and listened to my message.

During the altar call, she came forward to recommit her life to the Lord by repenting of her sins of contemplating suicide that night. She also repented of her sins of neglecting her ex-husband and children after the death of her daughter. God touched her marvelously and healed her broken heart that night. Eventually, she was accepted back into her family as she asked them to forgive her.

Unfortunately, as long as we are living in this cursed world, bad things can happen to God's good people. Therefore, God wrote in Romans 8:11, 35, 38-39, *"If God is for us, who can be against us? Who shall separate us from the love of Christ?* **Shall tribulation, or distress, or persecution, or famine, or nakedness, or peril, or sword?** *For I am persuaded that* **neither death nor life***, nor angels nor principalities nor powers, nor things present nor things to come, nor height nor depth, nor any other* *created thing,* **shall be able to separate us from the love of God which is in Christ Jesus our Lord."** According to the above Scriptures, even death cannot separate us from the love of God if we are in Jesus Christ. In a sense, when a saint physically dies on the earth, he or she will immediately be with the Lord in heaven to live with Him forever and ever.

Therefore, when we die in Christ on earth, we begin to really live with Him in eternity—even death shall not be able to separate us from the love of God. When we experience tribulations, sufferings and even death of a loved one, we must not blame God for that, but worship and praise Him even more just like Job did.

Regardless of what Satan did to us, we need to be very happy with our life in Christ and we must live our fully appointed life for His glory after spending a short season of grieving. Then the devil's intention to destroy us through the tragedies will be overcome by our testimonies of becoming more than conquerors in Christ.

JOB PLEADED AND REASONED WITH GOD

Throughout the rest of the Book of Job, he continuously pleaded and reasoned with God about the devastating tragedies that suddenly came upon him. Job believed that he hadn't committed any sins before God so he went through three stages of reasoning with the Lord:

1) **As a righteous man, he didn't know why he was struck with a sudden disaster** that destroyed all his possessions, servants and 10 children. In addition, he was severely afflicted with painful boils by Satan.

Unfortunately, while he was going through his unimaginable sufferings, Job cursed the day of his birth (Job 3:1) but he never denied God and His sovereignty. Even though Satan directly assaulted Job, he never addressed the devil throughout the whole book and he only poured out his sufferings before God. However, Job claimed in Chapter 3:25, *"For the thing I greatly feared has come upon me, and what I dreaded has happened to me."* According to the above Scripture, Job might have entertained a recurring fear of losing all his possessions including his 10 children.

What Job feared the most came upon him. We must not fill our hearts with the fear of losing what we love in this life. Fear in our hearts will open a door for the devil to attack us with his wicked schemes. Therefore, we read in 2 Timothy 1:7, *"For God has not given us a spirit of fear, but of power and of love and of a sound mind."*

2) **Job debated with his miserable comforters** (Job chapters 3-37): The main question of Job is *"Why the loving and all-powerful God allows the righteous one to suffer?"* However, Job's friends tried to convince him that God had judged and chastened him because of his sins and that his responses to them were coming from his self-righteousness. Up to chapter 37, Job tried to persuade them that he was innocent and righteous before God.

And he went on to declare that God was the One who had crushed him and loosed His hand to cut him off (Job 6:9). Job cried out to God in Job 7:20, *"Have I sinned? What have I done to You, O watcher of men? Why have You set me as Your target, so that I am a burden to myself?"* Throughout the debate with his friends, Job consistently professed that he was innocent before God.

3) **Finally, the Lord revealed His omnipotence and sovereignty** to Job in chapters 38-42: God challenged Job concerning his words without knowledge in Job 38:4, *"Where were you when I laid the foundations of the earth? Tell Me, if you have understanding."* The Lord continued His inquiry to Job in chapter 40:2, *"Shall the one who contends with the Almighty correct Him? He who rebukes God, let him answer it."* Finally, Job answered to God in Job 42:3b, 5-6, **"Therefore I have uttered what I did not understand...I have heard of You by the hearing of the ear, but now my eye sees You. Therefore I abhor myself, and repent in dust and ashes."**

And the Lord restored Job's losses when he prayed for his friends and He gave Job twice as much as he had before (Job 42:10). The Lord blessed Job's latter days more than his beginning. During the whole process of Job's struggles with the direct assaults of Satan, he never focused on him or directly launched any spiritual warfare against him. He only reasoned with God about his sufferings.

At the end, God dealt with Job by revealing His sovereignty over the whole of creation and his life. Ultimately, I believe that God allowed Job, a righteous man, to suffer for a season so that his testimony would encourage millions of God's children through the ages who have suffered from various assaults in their lives by Satan. During my 31 years of ministry in the nations, I also witnessed that God has allowed His righteous people to suffer or even to become martyrs for His glory so that their testimonies could encourage multitudes of other Christians.

SATAN TEMPTED KING DAVID TO SIN

In 1 Chronicles 21:1-4a, 7-18, 23-27, we can see the accounts of how Satan tempted King David to sin against God and how the Lord severely dealt with David's transgression. During the whole course of the event, King David never directly addressed or blamed Satan or fought against him. He only pleaded with the Lord for His divine mercy over his grievous sin. This account is another example of how the heroes of the Bible handled and managed the assaults of the devil—they never directly fought against him but they always turned to the Lord to assist them to deal with the power of darkness. Now let's examine the above Scriptures to see how King David handled his sin against God and how He dealt with him:

> **Now Satan stood up against Israel, and moved David to number Israel.** *So David said to Joab and to the leaders of the people, "Go, number Israel from Beersheba to Dan, and bring the number of them to me that I may know it." And Joab answered, "May the Lord make His people a hundred times more than they are. But, my lord the king, are they not all my lord's servants? Why then does my lord require this thing?* ***Why should he be a cause of guilt in Israel?"*** *Nevertheless the king's word prevailed against Joab. Therefore Joab departed and went throughout all Israel and came to Jerusalem.* (1 Chronicles 21:1-4) **And God was displeased with this thing; therefore**

He struck Israel.** So David said to God, "**I have sinned greatly, because I have done this thing; but now, I pray, take away the iniquity of Your servant, for I have done very foolishly**.*" Then the Lord spoke to Gad, David's seer, saying, "Go and tell David, saying, 'Thus says the Lord: I offer you three things; choose one of them for yourself, that I may do it to you.'" So Gad came to David and said to him, "Thus says the Lord: 'Choose for yourself, either three years of famine, or three months to be defeated by your foes with the sword of your enemies overtaking you, or else for three days the sword of the Lord—the plague in the land***, with the angel of the Lord destroying throughout all the territory of Israel.' Now consider what answer I should take back to Him who sent me."

And David said to Gad, "***I am in great distress. Please let me fall into the hand of the Lord, for His mercies are very great; but do not let me fall into the hand of man.*" So the Lord sent a plague upon Israel, and seventy thousand men of Israel fell. And God sent an angel to Jerusalem to destroy it**. As he was destroying, the Lord looked and relented of the disaster, and said to the angel who was destroying, "It is enough; now restrain your hand." And the angel of the Lord stood by the threshing floor of Ornan the Jebusite.

Then David lifted his eyes and saw the angel of the Lord standing between earth and heaven, having in his hand a drawn sword stretched out over Jerusalem. So David and the elders, clothed in sackcloth, fell on their faces. And David said to God, "Was it not I who commanded the people to be numbered? I am the one who has sinned and done evil *indeed; but these sheep, what have they done?* **Let Your hand, I pray, O Lord my God, be against me and my father's house, but not against Your people that they should be plagued.**" *Therefore, the angel of the Lord commanded Gad to say to David that David should go and erect an altar to the Lord on the threshing floor of Ornan the Jebusite.* (vss. 7-18)

But Ornan said to David, "Take it to yourself, and let my lord the king do what is good in his eyes. Look, I also give you the oxen for burnt offerings, the threshing implements for wood, and the wheat for the grain offering; I give it all." Then King David said to Ornan, "**No, but I will surely buy it for the full price, for I will not take what is yours for the Lord, nor offer burnt offerings with that which costs me nothing.**"

So David gave Ornan six hundred shekels of gold by weight for the place. And David built there an altar to the Lord, and offered burnt offerings and peace offerings, and called on the Lord; and **He answered him from heaven by fire on the altar of burnt offering.** *So the Lord commanded the angel, and he returned his sword to its sheath.* (vss. 23-27)

1) **David sinned against God by numbering Israel**: Following God's inauguration of David as the king over Israel, God blessed him and protected Israel from all surrounding nations. When they went to fight against invading enemy kings and their armies, it was God who fought for them and gave them victory. Therefore, God wanted King David to totally trust Him for the safety and protection of Israel and not rely on the number of soldiers that he accumulated over the years. Initially, Joab, the captain of the army of Israel, protested King David's request to number

Israel. However, David insisted for Joab to number the soldiers in Israel. Joab reported back to David that Israel had one million one hundred thousand men who drew the sword and Judah had four hundred and seventy thousand men who drew the sword (1 Chronicles 21:5). Satan wanted David to feel secure and proud of how many soldiers that he had trained instead of relying on God for the security of Israel. What David did displeased the Lord and He struck Israel with His judgment. We, the followers of Christ, also must not depend on our bank account, business, wealth, real estate or any other possessions or people as the sources of our safety, security and success, but only trust God as the provider, protector, sustainer and security of our lives.

2) **David repented before God:** David sincerely repented before God for his sins in 1 Chronicles 21:8, *"I have sinned greatly, because I have done this thing; but now, I pray, take away the iniquity of Your servant, for I have done very foolishly."* David didn't blame Satan for his sin nor did he try to fight against or bind the devil for how he enticed him to sin before God. Rather, he acknowledged his sin before God and asked His mercy. Just like David did, when we sin before God, we immediately need to run toward Him and ask His forgiveness and mercy. We must neither try to fight directly against the devil who deceived us nor reason with him about the deception so that we will not further fall into his evil plots.

3) **God began to punish David for his sin:** God offered three judgments from which David had to choose as a consequence of his sin in 1 Chronicles 21:11-12, *"Choose for yourself, either (1) three years of famine, or (2) three months to be defeated by your foes with the sword of your enemies overtaking you, or else (3) for three days the sword of the*

Lord—the plague in the land, with the angel of the Lord destroying throughout all the territory of Israel." David's response was to fall into the hand of the Lord in 1 Chronicles 21:13, *"I am in great distress. Please let me fall into the hand of the Lord, for His mercies are very great; but do not let me fall into the hand of man."* So the Lord sent a plague upon Israel, and seventy thousand men of Israel fell. And God sent an angel to destroy Jerusalem (vs. 14-15a).

David saw the angel of the Lord standing between earth and heaven, having in his hand a drawn sword stretched out over Jerusalem (vs. 16). Therefore, David and the elders clothed themselves in sackcloth and fell on their faces and said to the Lord (vs. 17), *"Was it not I who commanded the people to be numbered? I am the one who has sinned and done evil indeed; but these sheep, what have they done?* ***Let Your hand, I pray, O Lord my God, be against me and my father's house, but not against Your people that they should be plagued."***

We could see that David sincerely repented for his sins and he wanted God to punish him and his family rather than God's people in Jerusalem. This is a clear example of the fact that if the head of a nation sins before God, then the whole nation can also suffer the consequences. I believe that God punished David in order to warn the elders and leaders of Israel that if they sinned against Him, they would suffer His righteous judgment. Therefore, they should always fear God and not commit sin against Him again.

4) **The angel of the Lord directed David to erect the altar:** During the Old Testament days, in order for King David to atone for his sins, he had to offer burnt offerings and peace offerings before the presence of God. The Hebrew word for "burnt offering" actually means to "ascend," literally to "go up in smoke." In Leviticus 1:9 states, *"And the priest*

shall burn all on the altar as a burnt sacrifice, an offering made by fire, a sweet aroma to the Lord." A burnt offering was the complete destruction of the animal in an effort to renew the broken relationship between Holy God and sinful man.[13] After the burnt offerings, David was to present peace offerings that would invoke God's generous mercy and grace to pardon his sins.

5) **David erected the altar to the Lord:** David offered to purchase the threshing floor of Ornan the Jebusite but Ornan responded to him, *"Take it to yourself, and let my lord the king do what is good in his eyes. Look, I also give you the oxen for burnt offerings, the threshing implements for wood, and the wheat for the grain offering; I give it all."*

However, King David insisted that he would surely buy it for the full price, for he would neither take what was Ornan's for the Lord, nor offer burnt offerings with that which cost him nothing. David was a man of integrity and he would not want to offer anything to the Lord that didn't cost him anything. That means when we offer anything to the Lord, it also must cost us something significant.

6) **God accepted David's offerings and answered by fire:** When the Lord accepted David's offerings, He answered him by fire from heaven: *"David built there an altar to the Lord, and offered burnt offerings and peace offerings, and called on the Lord; and* **He answered him from heaven by fire on the altar of burnt offering**. *So the Lord commanded the angel, and he returned his sword to its sheath."* When God saw David's true repentant heart in action by building an altar, He accepted David's offerings and withdrew His judgment upon the Israelites in Jerusalem.

IF THE LORD IS NOT AMONG YOU, YOU WILL BE DEFEATED

It is obvious that if the Lord doesn't fight the battle against Satan and his wicked power of darkness for you, you will be utterly defeated according to Deuteronomy 1:42-44:

And the Lord said to me, "Tell them, 'Do not go up nor fight, for I am not among you; lest you be defeated before your enemies.'" "So I spoke to you; yet you would not listen, but rebelled against the command of the Lord, and presumptuously went up into the mountain. And the Amorites who dwelt in that mountain came out against you and chased you as bees do, and drove you back from Seir to Hormah."

Prior to the above Scriptures, Moses sent 12 men to spy out the Promised Land. Ten came back with a bad report and two (Joshua and Caleb) trusted the Lord and encouraged the Israelites to go up and possess the land. However, the Israelites complained before God and refused to enter the land God had given to them. Therefore, the anger of the Lord was manifested and He declared that the first generation of the men who came out of Egypt would all perish in the wilderness because of their rebellion.

After God's judgment had been pronounced to them, they again didn't obey God and went up into the mountain to fight the unauthorized battle against the Amorites. They were badly defeated before the enemy because the Lord was not with them. King David also had to learn his lesson for not totally relying on the Lord for deliverance from his enemies and, instead, trusting the might and numerical strength of his army.

In the case of King Saul, when he was afraid and his heart trembled greatly before the great army of the Philistines, he inquired of the Lord but He did not answer him (1 Samuel 28:4-6). Then Saul searched for a medium to conduct a séance for him, and Samuel appeared to him and pronounced his death (1 Samuel 28:18-19). Therefore, we, the children of God, must not launch any spiritual warfare against Satan or any power of darkness when the Lord is not with us and hasn't given us the authority to do so.

THE LORD REBUKE YOU, SATAN!

In the Book of Zechariah 3:1-5, 8, describes another event that took place in heaven in which Satan came up and stood before the Angel of the Lord to oppose Joshua the high priest:

> *Then he showed me Joshua the high priest standing before the Angel of the Lord, and **Satan standing at his right hand to oppose him. And the Lord said to Satan, "The Lord rebuke you, Satan! The Lord who has chosen Jerusalem rebuke you!** Is this not a brand plucked from the fire?" Now Joshua was clothed with filthy garments, and was standing before the Angel. Then He answered and spoke to those who stood before Him, saying, "Take away the filthy garments from him."*
>
> *And to him He said, "**See, I have removed your iniquity from you, and I will clothe you with rich robes.**" And I said, "Let them put a clean turban on his head." **So they put a clean turban on his head, and they put the clothes on him**. And the Angel of the Lord stood by." "Hear, O Joshua, the high priest, You*

*and your companions who sit before you, for they are a wondrous sign; for behold, **I am bringing forth My Servant the BRANCH.***"

Could Joshua, the High Priest, who was standing before the Angel of the Lord with filthy garments, be representing Jesus Christ who took the sin of the world upon His body? Since God called Joshua "My Servant the BRANCH," the above Scriptures definitely imply that Satan somehow came up to the presence of the Angel of the Lord to oppose Joshua—the Lamb of God who took away the sin of the world. We have already discussed the fact that Lucifer who had been judged by God and was cast out of heaven. This happened at some point prior to the above-mentioned encounter with Joshua, the High Priest. Of course, the Angel of the Lord had the power to bind Satan and cast him into the eternal lake of fire when he opposed Joshua in His presence.

However, even the Angel of the Lord was not able to bind Satan and cast him away forever prior to his appointed time in Revelation 20:1-3. If He had bound Satan and cast him into the abyss in Zechariah 3:1-5, then all those souls that needed to be saved following the resurrection of the Lord Jesus Christ would not have a chance to hear the gospel. Therefore, the Lord simply declared in Zechariah 3:2, *"The Lord rebuke you, Satan! The Lord who has chosen Jerusalem rebuke you!"*

My point is this: if the Lord Himself will not bind Satan before his appointed time, then what makes us, the believers in Christ, think that we can bind Satan with our own authority prior to his designated time of judgment? When Satan assaults the children of God, then we can say to him just what is said in Zechariah 3:2—*"The Lord rebuke you, Satan!"* When we invoke the name of the Lord to rebuke Satan, then he has to directly deal with God who we totally depend on for spiritual warfare. The result is that Satan is no match for the

Lord Himself and he will flee from us as we call upon the name of God to rebuke him. The Lord restored Joshua, the High Priest, to His victorious position of authority in verse 5, *"See, I have removed your iniquity from you, and I will clothe you with rich robes. Let them put a clean turban on his head. So they put a clean turban on his head, and they put the clothes on him. And the Angel of the Lord stood by."* Therefore, Joshua, described as wearing filthy garments, was the prophetic picture of Jesus Christ who took the sin of the world on the cross. But Jesus Christ was resurrected and clothed in royal robes as the Messiah of the Jews and Gentiles of the world—*My Servant the BRANCH.*

THE LORD SENT MOSES TO PHARAOH

Following his encounter with the Lord in Exodus 3:2-6, Moses was led by the power of God to perform ten miracles before Pharaoh. Through the demonstration of the power of God, eventually Pharaoh released the Israelites from Egyptian bondage after 430 years of slavery. God solemnly declared what He would do to Egyptians in Exodus 3:20, *"So I will stretch out My hand and strike Egypt with all My wonders which I will do in its midst; and after that he (Pharaoh) will let you go."*

Throughout the course of Moses' encounters with Pharaoh, the sorcerers and magicians of Egypt, he never tried to fight his spiritual warfare against Satan, the principality over Egypt, and the evil powers of darkness. However, Moses repeatedly came before the Lord and totally depended on His wisdom, authority and power to deal with the satanic power of darkness that controlled Pharaoh and the Egyptian kingdom. When Moses encountered stiff opposition from

Pharaoh, he simply sought God's instructions and demonstrated the power of God to defeat the tactics of the enemy. In fact, Moses never paid any attention to the demonic powers that controlled Pharaoh and his kingdom.

The ultimate petition of Moses was written in Exodus 33:13-14, *"Now therefore, I pray, if I have found grace in Your sight,* **show me now Your way, that I may know You and that I may find grace in Your sight.** *And consider that this nation is Your people."* And He said, **"My presence will go with you, and I will give you rest."** Moses' constant desire during the journey of the exodus was to know the way of the Lord so that he could totally rely on God to defeat the wicked schemes of the devil. The response to Moses' request was given by the Lord in verse 14, *"My presence will go with you, and I will give you rest."*

When the Lord's presence goes with you, He will fight the battle for you against Satan and his wicked demonic forces of darkness. So the ministry of spiritual warfare belongs to the Lord and it is not yours. All you have to do is to listen to the guidance of the Lord and simply obey His every direction—in so doing; you will find rest in Him. Remember, the battle belongs to the Lord! God simply desires His children to obey His voice according to Exodus 15:26, then they can find rest and receive His divine health:

> *If you diligently* **heed the voice of the Lord** *your God and* **do what is right in His sight, give ear to His commandments and keep all His statutes,** *I will put none of the diseases on you which I have brought on the Egyptians.* **For I am the Lord who heals you.**

As we obey God's voice, commandments, statutes, and do what is right in His sight, He will fight the battle for us and bring healing and deliverance during our journey of this life.

That means, we do not need to focus on battling with Satan and his wicked powers of darkness each day, but totally trust and rely on God's authority and power by magnifying His name with praise and thanksgiving in our hearts. Then God will protect us as Psalm 91 promises and He will fight the battle against Satan and his wicked evil powers of darkness as we totally rest in Him each day.

JOSHUA'S VICTORY AT JERICHO

Before Joshua ever engaged in his battle against Jericho, God already promised him victory by declaring in Joshua 6:2, *"See! I have given Jericho into your hand, its king, and the mighty men of valor."* Therefore, Joshua knew that the Lord guaranteed the victory in the fight against Jericho so he just needed to carefully observe the instruction of the Lord in Joshua 6:3-5:

> *You shall march around the city, all you men of war; you shall go all around the city once. This you shall do six days. And seven priests shall bear seven trumpets of rams' horns before the ark.* **But the seventh day you shall march around the city seven times, and the priests shall blow the trumpets.** *It shall come to pass, when they make a long blast with the ram's horn,* **and when you hear the sound of the trumpet, that all the people shall shout with a great shout; then the wall of the city will fall down flat.** *And the people shall go up every man straight before him.*

When we examine the above Scriptures, we can see that God gave Joshua and the Israelites very specific instructions for him to follow in order to defeat the enemy. If Joshua didn't obey the exact direction of the Lord, then he wouldn't have won the victory over Jericho. And he declared in Joshua 6:17a, *"Now the city shall be doomed by the Lord to destruction, it and all who are in it."* Joshua was clearly stating that the Lord would bring the destruction of Jericho according to His own word in Joshua 6:2. Joshua put his total trust in the Lord who would fight the battle for him. The fulfillment of the above victory was materialized in Joshua 6:15-21:

> *But it came to pass on the seventh day that they rose early, about the dawning of the day, and* **marched around the city seven times** *in the same manner. On that day only they marched around the city seven times. And the seventh time it happened, when the priests blew the trumpets, that Joshua said to the people:* **"Shout, for the Lord has given you the city! Now the city shall be doomed by the Lord to destruction, it and all who are in it.**
>
> *Only Rahab the harlot shall live, she and all who are with her in the house, because she hid the messengers that we sent.* **And you, by all means abstain from the accursed things, lest you become accursed when you take of the accursed things, and make the camp of Israel a curse, and trouble it.** *But all the silver and gold, and vessels of bronze and iron, are consecrated to the Lord; they shall come into the treasury of the Lord."*
>
> *So the people shouted when the priests blew the trumpets. And it happened when the people heard the sound of the trumpet, and* **the people shouted with a**

great shout, that the wall fell down flat. *Then the people went up into the city, every man straight before him, and they took the city. And they utterly destroyed all that was in the city, both man and woman, young and old, ox and sheep and donkey, with the edge of the sword.*

Since Joshua and the Israelites obeyed God's exact instructions in their fight against the city of Jericho, He utterly destroyed the city for them. Throughout the battles against the inhabitants in the Promise Land, Joshua had to exactly follow the guidance of the Lord in order to prevail. During the course of Joshua's battles, God never directed him to launch spiritual warfare against the principalities or powers of the air or the evil forces of darkness or Satan directly.

Instead, Joshua was instructed by the Lord to absolutely depend on Him for the warfare against his enemies. He knew that the battle belonged to the Lord. Likewise, when we engage in any spiritual battle against the power of darkness, we need to go directly to the Lord in prayer and fasting to know His perfect will for the situation. Then, we must obey and follow the guidance of the Holy Spirit to defeat every scheme of the devil by trusting Him.

I COME IN THE NAME OF THE LORD OF HOSTS

We can learn how David fought against Goliath in his epic spiritual and physical battle in 1 Samuel Chapter 17. The Scriptures describe how Goliath, the Philistine giant, equipped with mighty armor, taunted the Israelites in verses 4-10 with his pompous words:

*And a champion went out from the camp of the Philistines, named Goliath, from Gath, **whose height was six cubits and a span. He had a bronze helmet on his head, and he was armed with a coat of mail, and the weight of the coat was five thousand shekels of bronze. And he had bronze armor on his legs and a bronze javelin between his shoulders. Now the staff of his spear was like a weaver's beam, and his iron spearhead weighed six hundred shekels; and a shield-bearer went before him.***

*Then he stood and cried out to the armies of Israel and said to them, "Why have you come out to line up for battle? Am I not a Philistine, and you the servants of Saul? Choose a man for yourselves, and let him come down to me. If he is able to fight with me and kill me, then we will be your servants. But if I prevail against him and kill him, then you shall be our servants and serve us." And the Philistine said, "**I defy the armies of Israel this day; give me a man, that we may fight together.**"*

You can see according to the above Scriptures that Goliath was a giant wearing full protective gear as he was challenging and mocking King Saul and the armies of Israel. Unfortunately, when Saul and all Israel heard the words of Goliath, they were greatly dismayed and afraid (vs. 11). Meanwhile, David was sent by his father Jesse to take some supplies to his three older brothers who were serving in Saul's army. While the armies of Israel were totally terrified by the presence and arrogant words of Goliath, David had a different spirit by asking, *"What shall be done for the man who kills this Philistine and takes away the reproach from Israel?"* However, Eliab, his oldest brother, heard David speaking with the men and his anger was aroused against David and he said,

"Why did you come down here? And with whom have you left those few sheep in the wilderness? I know your pride and the insolence of your heart, for you have come down to see the battle (vs. 28)." Then David gave the following answer in verse 29, *"What have I done now? Is there not a cause?"* When one is anointed by the Lord to engage in His battle against the evil forces of darkness, one's own family member can rise up against him or her. If that happens, one needs to focus on one's eyes on the Lord and His cause and press on to obey His commands.

As Goliath was taunting the armies of Israel, David saw the cause to rise up and fight against him. When David came to Saul, he said to him in verse 32, *"Let no man's heart fail because of him; your servant will go and fight with this Philistine."* Unfortunately, Saul—the ex-anointed King just as Eliab had done, didn't realize that the Spirit of the Lord was upon David and said in verse 33, *"You are not able to go against this Philistine to fight with him; for you are a youth, and he a man of war from his youth."*

However, David had already won the victory over Goliath in his heart before he even attempted to fight him by declaring his battle-outcome in verse 36, *"Your servant has killed both lion and bear; and this uncircumcised Philistine will be like one of them, seeing he has defied the armies of the living God."* Regardless of what King Saul said about Goliath, David claimed and displayed his confidence in the Lord. Saul tried to clothe David with his armor—a bronze helmet for his head and with a coat of mail for his chest. But David wasn't even able to walk with such heavy armor on so he took it off.

Perhaps we can say that Saul's armor symbolizes manmade devises such as religious tools, traditions, rituals and teachings that do not have the anointing of the Holy Spirit. We are also not able to fight and prevail against the power of darkness by putting on someone else's armor, or by imitating their instructions based on reading their spiritual warfare books or teachings or attending their seminars. We can only defeat the works of the devil by totally depending on the power of the Holy Spirit that has been authorized by the authority of Jesus Christ. We can never prevail against the power of Satan if we do spiritual warfare that has not been authorized according to the written word of God. David, who had been anointed with the power of the Holy Spirit to become the next king of the Israelites, declared that the Lord would fight the battle for him. David knew that it was God's divinely appointed time for him to rise up and defeat Goliath. Because David had the assurance that the Lord would deliver Goliath into his hand in 1 Samuel 17:45-47:

Then David said to the Philistine, "You come to me with a sword, with a spear, and with a javelin. **But I come to you in the name of the Lord of hosts, the God of the armies of Israel, whom you have defied.** *This day the Lord will deliver you into my hand, and I will strike you and take your head from you. And this day I will give the carcasses of the camp of the Philistines to the birds of the air and the wild beasts of the earth, that* **all the earth may know that there is a God in Israel. Then all this assembly shall know that the Lord does not save with sword and spear; for the battle is the Lord's, and He will give you into our hands."**

David never addressed Satan and his power of darkness throughout his life's battles against the enemies of God. But he totally depended on the mighty power of the Lord and the anointing of the Holy Spirit that was upon him to be victorious in every battle in his life. Therefore, we can conclude that David was definitely led by the Lord to fight against Goliath because he declared the victory before he ever engaged in his battle against the giant by declaring—*for the battle is the Lord's, and He will give you into our hands.*

Likewise, we must always remember that any spiritual battles the enemy launches against us belong to the Lord and we simply need to follow His direction to achieve the victory. We can confidently declare, *"If God is for us, who can be against us?* (Romans 8:31b)" However, if God is not with us, then we will be alone to fight the battle and will be in great trouble.

KING JEHOSHAPHAT'S VICTORY

When King Jehoshaphat faced the large coalition of the people of Moab, Ammon and others that came to battle against him, he set himself to seek the Lord and proclaimed a fast throughout all Judah in 2 Chronicles 20:2-3 and he cried out to the Lord for help:

> *Then some came and told Jehoshaphat, saying, "A great multitude is coming against you from beyond the sea, from Syria; and they are in Hazazon Tamar" (which is En Gedi). And **Jehoshaphat feared, and set himself to seek the Lord, and proclaimed a fast throughout all Judah.***

When Jehoshaphat feared the invading armies, he humbled himself and began to seek the Lord by proclaiming a fast throughout all Judah. Because he realized that he could have victory over the great multitudes of enemies only if the Lord would fight the battle for them, so he confessed in 2 Chronicles 20:12, *"O our God, will You not judge them? For we have no power against this great multitude that is coming against us; nor do we know what to do,* **but our eyes are upon You.**"

In the same way, in order for any believers to have victory over the power of darkness, their eyes must be fixed on the Lord and Him alone. As Jehoshaphat put his total trust in God and God alone, the Lord answered his prayer in 2 Chronicles 20:15, 17, "**Do not be afraid nor dismayed** *because of this great multitude,* **for the battle in not yours, but God's.** *You will not need to fight in this battle. Position yourselves,* **stand still and see the salvation of the Lord, who is with you, O Judah and Jerusalem!** *Do not fear or be dismayed; tomorrow go out against them,* **for the Lord is with you.**"

Of course, the power of darkness influences each situation behind every physical battle in life. The devil causes us to believe that the battle will be unbearable and too fearful for us to manage with our own strength. But, as we put our faith in the Lord, trusting that the battle belongs to Him, then He will fight against the wicked schemes of Satan for us. We only need to stand still and see the salvation of the Lord moving on behalf of our petitions. If God is for us, who can be against us? According to God's instruction, King Jehoshaphat sent out the worship team to sing unto the Lord before the army in 2 Chronicles 20:21-22:

> *And when he had consulted with the people,* **he appointed those who should sing to the Lord, and who should praise the beauty of holiness**, *as they went out before the army and were saying: "Praise the Lord, for His mercy endures forever." Now* **when they began to sing and to praise, the Lord set ambushes** *against the people of Ammon, Moab, and Mount Seir, who had come against Judah; and* **they were defeated.**

When we focus on great dangers, the attacks of Satan, and the threats of the enemy, we can become paralyzed with fear. However, instead of allowing spirits of fear to control our hearts and minds, we can fix our eyes on God by praising and trusting Him to fight the battles for us. When Jehoshaphat's worshippers began to sing and praise the Lord before the vast invading armies, the Lord rose up and set ambushes and defeated the multitudes of enemies.

Once again, Jehoshaphat was never instructed to fight directly against Satan and the principalities behind the enemy forces, but to put his total trust in the power of God. Therefore, when you are struggling with a big problem in life, you must not tell God how big the trouble you are facing is, rather, tell your big issues how big God is. Just like Jehoshaphat did, you can ignore Satan and the power of darkness behind the attack and focus on the Lord and praise Him until He will move on your behalf. Then the Lord will fight the battle for you and you will always be protected by Him in victory.

EXAMPLES OF RIGHT SPIRITUAL WARFARE SCRIPTURES IN PSALMS

King David, the Psalmist, was a great warrior as well as an anointed worshipper throughout his journey of leading the Israelites. He had to constantly escape the threat of King Saul and engage in numerous battles during his reign over Judah and Israel. Regardless of the magnitude of the enemy's attacks in David's life, he always put his total trust in the Lord because he knew that the battles belong to Him.

Therefore, David never focused on Satan or his wicked power of darkness during his struggles and battles, but he totally depended on the Lord to bring His victory for the Israelites—His chosen people. As we examine the following Scriptures, we will be able to learn **how to conduct spiritual warfare correctly by totally trusting and relying on God and resting in Him:**

- Psalm 18:3, 13-14, 17, 20, 39, 46, ***"I will call upon the Lord, who is worthy to be praised; so shall I be saved from my enemies...The Lord thundered from heaven, and the Most High uttered His voice, hailstones and coals of fire. He sent out His arrows and scattered the foe, lightnings in abundance, and He vanquished them...He delivered me from my strong enemy, from those who hated me, for they were too strong for me...The Lord rewarded me according to my righteousness; according to the cleanness of my hands He has recompensed me...For You have armed me with strength for the battle; You have subdued under me those who rose up against me...The Lord lives! Blessed be my Rock! Let the God of my salvation be exalted."***

It is obvious that King David called upon the Lord in praise whenever his enemies rose against him. His spiritual warfare tactic against the power of darkness behind his enemies was to completely depend on the Lord to fight the battle and to bring him victory. King David recognized that it was the Lord who delivered him from the strong enemies that were too powerful for him to defeat.

Therefore, David praised the Lord and acknowledged Him by singing—***"The Lord lives! Blessed be my Rock! Let the God of my salvation be exalted."*** We need to realize that Satan is no match for God if He rises up and fights the battle for us. If we dwell in the presence and glory of God, then His light will destroy any wicked schemes of the devil for our lives. Therefore, we need to praise God and declare His glory over any situations in our lives that have been affected by the devil. As we do so He will defeat every evil plan, attack, intention and scheme for us.

- Psalm 23:1, 3-6, *"The Lord is my shepherd; I shall not want...He restores my soul; He leads me in the paths of righteousness for His name's sake. Yea, though I walk through the valley of the shadow of death, I will fear no evil; for You are with me; Your rod and Your staff, they comfort me. You prepare a table before me in the presence of my enemies; You anoint my head with oil; my cup runs over. Surely goodness and mercy shall follow me all the days of my life; and I will dwell in the house of the Lord forever."*

King David depended on the Lord as a sheep would totally rely on the shepherd so he could say, *"I shall not want* [chaser in Hebrew: lacking, be needed, be deprived]." He further declared that he would fear no evil even though he would walk through the valley of the shadow of death. As David utterly put his absolute trust in the Lord who would defend and fight for him, he was confidently able to say— *"Surely goodness and mercy shall follow me all the days of my life."*

We can learn from David's example to know how to absolutely rely on God for any spiritual warfare we may face during the journey of our lives. Our focus must be on the mighty power of God and not on the power of the devil. The more we focus on the devil, the more fearful we will be of the evil forces of darkness. But when we fix our eyes on the goodness of God and His faithfulness, then His divine peace will guard our hearts and minds in Christ. We can rest in His divine presence, favor, provisions, and victory.

- Psalm 27:1, 3, 4-6, "**The Lord is my light and my salvation** [*yesha* in Hebrew: it means deliverance, rescue, salvation, safety, welfare, etc.]; **whom shall I fear? The Lord is the strength of my life; of whom shall I be afraid?** *Though an army should encamp against me, my heart shall not fear; though war should rise against me, in this I will be confident. One thing I have desired of the Lord, that will I seek:* **that I may dwell in the house of the Lord all the days of my life, to behold the beauty of the Lord,** *and to inquire in His temple. For in the time of trouble He shall hide me in His pavilion; in the secret place of His tabernacle He shall hide me;* **He shall set me high upon a rock. And now my head shall be lifted up above my enemies all around me; therefore I will offer sacrifices of joy in His tabernacle; I will sing, yes, I will sing praises to the Lord.**"

According to the above Scriptures, we can see clearly that King David put his total trust in the Lord over any spiritual battles that he had to face. His confidence was rested totally in the Lord by declaring, "*The Lord is my light and my salvation; whom shall I fear?*" He didn't fear Satan, demons, powers of darkness or men and never directly engaged in spiritual warfare against the devil and his wicked demonic spirits.

We also need to put our total trust in the Lord and declare His goodness like King David did—*my head shall be lifted up above my enemies all around me; therefore I will offer sacrifices of joy in His tabernacle; I will sing praises to the Lord.* When we do that, we will ignore the devil and his wicked evil plots because our eyes will be focused on God and His mighty power, faithfulness, love, joy, peace, mercy, grace, and blessings.

- Psalm 68:1, 2b, 3, 17, 19-20, "*Let God arise, let His enemies be scattered; let those also who hate Him flee before Him...As wax melts before the fire, so let the wicked perish at the presence of God. But let the righteous be glad; let them rejoice before God; yes, let them rejoice exceedingly...The chariots of God are twenty thousand, even thousands of thousands; the Lord is among them as in Sinai, in the Holy Place...Blessed be the Lord who daily loads us with benefits, the God of our salvation! Our God is the God of salvation; and to God the Lord belong escapes from death.*"

The secret of King David's success in spiritual warfare rested on his asking God to arise over his battles as he relied on His presence to scatter his enemies. He wasn't fighting against the powers of darkness with his own strength or strategies or skills. Rather, he fought his enemies by invoking God's presence to defeat them and cause them to perish. As we depend on God to fight our spiritual battles by praising and rejoicing in His presence, He will deliver us from the many traps of the devil—even from death.

Likewise, if we praise the Lord and dwell in His presence in the midst of our spiritual battles, the God of our salvation will disperse the power of darkness and bring His deliverance and victory in our lives.

- Psalm 91:1-3, 5-7, 9-11, "*He who dwells in the secret place of the Most High shall abide under the shadow of the Almighty. I will say of the Lord, 'He is my*

*refuge and my fortress; My God, **in Him I will trust**.'*
*Surely He shall deliver you from the snare of the fowler and from the perilous pestilence...**You shall not be afraid of terror by night, nor of the arrow that flies by day, nor of the pestilence that walks in darkness, nor of the destruction that lays waste at noonday.***
*A thousand may fall at your side and ten thousand at your right hand; but it shall not come near you...**Because you have made the Lord, who is my refuge, even the Most High, your dwelling place, no evil shall befall you**, nor shall any plague come near your dwelling; for He shall give His angels charge over you, to keep you in all your ways."*

Once again, King David's secret to winning spiritual warfare against his numerous enemies was to dwell in the secret place of the Most High God by declaring *"**In Him I will trust!**"* Because he made the Lord as his refuge and dwelling place, he was confidently able to declare that no evil would befall him. He further goes on to say that God would give His angels charge over him and keep him safe in all his ways.

Therefore, when we are facing attacks from the devil, instead of directly trying to launch spiritual warfare against him, we should call upon the name of the Lord and ask His presence to cover us so that no evil would befall on us all the days of our lives. If we try to fight against Satan with our own strength and understanding, we will be no match for his wicked power and schemes. However, the Lord fights the battle for us because we trust His glory, presence, authority and power. As we do so, Satan will be no match for the living God. When Psalm 91's protection and promises cover us, Satan will not have any power over us all the days of our life.

- Psalm 121:2-3, 5, 7-8, *"My help comes from the Lord, who made heaven and earth. He will not allow your foot to be moved; He who keeps you will not slumber... The Lord is your keeper; the Lord is your shade at your right hand... The Lord shall preserve you from all evil: He shall preserve your soul. The Lord shall preserve your going out and your coming in from this time forth, and even forevermore."*

As we examine the above Psalm, we can clearly identify that King David knew without doubt that his help came from the Lord as the Keeper of his life. He confidently declared that the Lord would preserve him from all evil. That means David utterly depended on God to preserve him from his every spiritual and physical battle in his life. If the Lord fights the battle for you, you can also assuredly say that the Lord shall preserve your going out and your coming in from this time forth, and even forevermore. Amen!

- Psalm 150:2, 5, *"Praise Him for His mighty acts; praise Him according to His excellent greatness... Let everything that has breath praise the Lord."*

Finally, King David's great strength and victory over all of his enemies and power of darkness rested in his constant desire to praise the Lord according to His excellent greatness. No matter what happened during the journey of David's life, he constantly praised the Lord for his divine victory, life, strength, courage, anointing, wisdom, and blessings. When the powers of darkness surround you with demonic fear, discouragement, doubt, worries, anxiety, negative thoughts, bitterness, depressions, oppressions, self-condemnation, self-judgment, self-pity, and the like, you need to praise the Lord until His glory and presence fills your heart and mind.

When God's presence fills your life with His glory, all your fears will dissipate immediately and you will find His divine peace that will lead you to spiritual victory over Satan's assaults. Therefore, when you are engaging in any spiritual battles against Satan and his powers of darkness, you need to praise the Lord regardless of how the enemies try to bring great fear in your heart. You must not directly engage in fighting with Satan or his wicked evil forces of darkness with your own tactics or understandings based on reading spiritual warfare books.

If you launch your offensive spiritual warfare against Satan against the will of the Lord, then you can be severely attacked by the enemy. However, if you invoke the Lord's presence and glory to fill your heart by totally ignoring the threats of the devil and begin to praise Him and to rely on Him to destroy the works of the evil one, then He will fight the battle for you. When the bright light of God overshadows you, then no power of darkness can hold on to you. His light will swallow up the darkness of Satan around you and as you resist him, he will flee from you.

ARCHANGEL MICHAEL FOUGHT AGAINST THE PRINCE OF THE KINGDOM OF PERSIA

Daniel, one of the minor prophets of the Old Testament, was a righteous man. In Daniel 9:20, he was praying and confessing his sins and the sins of his people Israel by petitioning his supplication before the Lord his God. While he was praying, the archangel Gabriel came to speak to him in Daniel 9:21, *"yes, while I was speaking in prayer, the man Gabriel, whom I had seen in the vision at the beginning, being caused to fly swiftly, reached me about the time of the evening offering."* Another time, Daniel mourned and fasted for three full weeks and lifted up his prayers before the Lord (Daniel 10:2-3). While he was deep in prayer, an angel came and touched him and began to reveal the kind of spiritual warfare that was going on in the heavenly realm in Daniel 10:12-13, 19-20:

> *Then he said to me, "Do not fear, Daniel, **for from the first day that you set your heart to understand,** and to humble yourself before your God, your words were heard; and I have come because of your words. **But the prince of the kingdom of Persia withstood me twenty-one days**; and behold, Michael, one of the chief princes, came to help me, for I had been left alone there with the kings of Persia.*
>
> *And he said, **"O man greatly beloved, fear not! Peace be to you; be strong, yes, be strong!"** So when he spoke to me I was strengthened, and said, "Let my lord speak, for you have strengthened me." Then he said, "Do you know why I have come to you? **And now I must return to fight with the prince of Persia**; and when I have gone forth, indeed the prince of Greece will come.*

The angel revealed the secret warfare that was going on in the heavenly realms from the first day that Daniel began to pray for a total of 21 days. The angel assured Daniel that God heard his prayers the first day he prayed and he was dispatched to Daniel because of his prayers. However, as the angel was probably passing through the second heavenly realm where the powers and principalities dwell, the prince of the kingdom of Persia (the principality ruling in the kingdom of Persia) withstood him for 21 days. That means, even though the angel was dispatched on the first day of Daniel's prayer, he was not able to get through the line of defense of the principality of Persia for 21 days. In this point we need to realize that even the mighty angel who was sent by the Lord had to face strong resistance from the prince of the kingdom of Persia for 21 days. That means we, the children of God, can also face severe opposition from the evil forces of darkness when we begin to pray for God to move on our behalf. In Daniel's case, regardless of what the angel told him about the spiritual warfare that was going on in the second heavenly realm, he never directly fought against the principality of Persia. He simply directed his prayers to God and He dispatched the angelic forces of Gabriel and Michael to deal with the prince of the kingdom of Persia.

Therefore, the lesson for us from this account is that as children of God, we need only to sincerely pray to the Lord over any troubling matters, situations, circumstances and people in our lives or over our nation or in the world. Then God will hear our prayers and dispatch His angels to deal with the principalities, powers, the rulers of the darkness of this age and spiritual hosts of wickedness **in the heavenly places** that are blocking us from receiving His answers **in the earthly realms**.

It is not our domain to fight against the principalities in the second heavenly realm by binding them or casting them out in the name of Jesus Christ. If we do that we are engaging in an unauthorized battle against the very powerful demonic forces in the air and they can come and tear us apart with their wicked evil power. We can pray with total faith and trust in the Lord, and then He will fight the battle for us. We can see the salvation of the Lord moving in victory on behalf of our prayers as we wait upon Him.

As we bring to a close on our study of how the Old Testament heroes dealt with the satanic power of darkness, we can conclude that they never directly addressed or fought against Satan or the principalities, and powers of the darkness in the heavenly places. **There is not a single Scripture in the Old Testament in which the Lord suggested or directed His chosen priests, prophets or kings to bind Satan and his hosts of evil powers of darkness when they were attacked.**

They totally depended on the Lord to fight the battles for them. Likewise, we must also rely on God's mighty presence and power to defeat every evil attack of the devil in our journey of life on the earth. If we dwell in the secret place of the Most High God, then we will abide under the shadow of the Almighty. As the Lord becomes our refuge and our fortress by totally trusting Him, then He will surely deliver us from every wicked plan of the devil all the days of our lives. Let our focus on spiritual warfare be to magnify the Lord and not on the devil. Satan has been already defeated, cast out of heaven, and is waiting to be thrown into the eternal lake of fire in the future. If God is with us, then no weapon formed against us shall prosper or succeed in our lives.

Chapter 5

DEALING WITH SATAN IN THE NEW TESTAMENT

Now we will examine the New Testament Scriptures to find out exactly how the Lord Jesus Christ and the Apostles direct us to handle spiritual warfare correctly. We will also identify the Scriptures that many spiritual warfare teachers have used to misguide their followers on how to fight against the power of darkness. They normally teach their disciples to engage in direct confrontation against Satan, principalities, powers, rulers of the darkness of this age, and spiritual hosts of wickedness **in the heavenly places** in the name of Jesus Christ.

We will also discuss the consequences of engaging in unauthorized spiritual warfare against Satan and his wicked evil powers of darkness in the heavenly realms. I would like to suggest for anyone who is reading this book that you have your heart and mind open to examine Scripture like the Bereans did in Acts 17:11, *"These* (Bereans) *were more fair-minded than those in Thessalonica, in that they received the word with all readiness, and searched the Scriptures daily to find out whether these things were so."* Therefore, I pray that you will carefully study all the Scriptures, including the correct meanings of Greek words, which I recommend in this book to understand the true teachings of the spiritual warfare in the New Testament. If there were anyone who had the power to bind Satan in the world, it would have been the Son of the living God, Jesus Christ. However, when He encountered Satan's temptations, He didn't bind him and his evil powers of darkness but He simply rebuked him by saying "It is written!" Jesus Christ knows very well that an angel will bind Satan and cast him into the bottomless pit for 1,000 years in Revelation 20:1-3 and that eventually he will be forever cast into the lake of fire in Revelation 20:10.

That means that the Father God has appointed a time and date for Satan and his fallen angels to be bound and cast into the lake of fire according to His perfect will. Therefore, no one including the Archangel Michael or even Jesus Christ can bind Satan before his appointed time and cast him into the bottomless pit or the lake of fire. If Jesus Christ would have bound Satan and cast him into the lake of fire when he first encountered him in Matthew 4:1, then he could not have fulfilled His mission of dying on the cross and being resurrected to be the Savior of fallen mankind.

And generations of the lost souls up to that day would have fallen into the eternal lake of fire prematurely. Jesus Christ came to fulfill Father God's perfect will to deliver fallen mankind from the slavery of Satan and from the eternal lake of fire. We can see in Matthew 8:28-29 that demons would try to reason with Jesus Christ if He had come to torture them before God's appointed time:

> *When Jesus arrived on the other side of the lake, in the region of the Gadarenes, two men who were possessed by demons met him. They came out of the tombs and were so violent that no one could go through that area. They began screaming at him, "Why are you interfering with us, Son of God? Have*

you come here to torture us **before God's appointed time?**" (NLT)

Therefore, demons also know they have an appointed time to be cast into the lake of fire. Until then they have the legal right to stay on the earth according to God's perfect will. That means, even Jesus Christ couldn't bind demons and throw them into the bottomless pit or the lake of fire before their appointed time. Thus, Jesus Christ simply cast them out of the demon possessed men and allowed them to go into the herd of swine in Matthew 8:32. **Once they were cast out of the men, they would be freed to roam around in the region to find another targeted victim to possess until their appointed time in Revelation 20:1-3 and 10 is fulfilled.**

However, according to the instruction of many spiritual warfare teachers, they mislead many of their followers to believe that any believer in Christ has absolute authority to bind Satan and all the powers of darkness in the heavenly realms whenever and wherever they can. In reality, only Jesus Christ has all authority in heaven and on earth in Matthew 28:18. Christians can only exercise Jesus Christ's delegated authority that has been authorized in the Scriptures.

Even Jesus Christ declares in John 5:19, "***The Son can do nothing of Himself, but what He sees the Father do;*** *for whatever He does, the Son also does in like manner."* Likewise, Jesus Christ also states in John 15:5, "*I am the vine, you are the branches. He who abides in Me, and I in him, bears much fruit;* ***for without Me you can do nothing****."* As Christians, we can only do what we see Jesus Christ doing through us—we can only do what we are permitted to do according to His delegated authority in the Bible.

However, many spiritual warfare teachers guide their followers to bind Satan over their lives, homes, businesses, churches, and even over the whole city, region or nation. If we truly have the power to bind Satan, principalities, powers, the rulers of the darkness of this age, and spiritual hosts of wickedness **in the heavenly places** in the name of Jesus Christ, then immediately the whole region, city or world should be totally freed from any of their evil influences. However, do we really experience total freedom from every wicked scheme of Satan when we bind him and cast him into the bottomless pit or the lake of fire against the appointed time and will of God? That never happens. In reality, Satan who also knows the Scriptures can come against those who directly fight against him and tear them apart with his wicked evil power. Be Aware!

Until the Holy Spirit corrected me about my incorrect ways of doing spiritual warfare, I was also deeply influenced by the misguided teachings of many spiritual warfare books that I had read. One time I was ministering in Nepal with a very well known spiritual warfare teacher and writer. He was ministering to around 200 Nepalese pastors and leaders with his ways of doing spiritual warfare. He was teaching them to bind Satan and all his powers of darkness ruling over the capital city of Katmandu and over all of Nepal in the name of Jesus Christ. He even suggested that they go around the Hindu and Buddhist temples and bind all demonic powers of darkness and cast them out into the bottomless pit in Christ's name.

One night after the conference session was over, I came back to my hotel room around 9:30 p. m. after having dinner with the spiritual warfare teacher. I was in my room for about 10 minutes when I felt a very powerful demonic presence—it could have been Satan himself. All of a sudden, the light in my room went out and I began to feel the indescribable evil power of darkness in the room. I began to bind Satan and all the evil powers in the room in the name of Jesus Christ and I commanded them to go to the pit of hell. I was engaged in spiritual warfare directly against Satan for over 30 minutes, but he didn't budge no matter how hard I commanded him to go to the pit of hell where he rightly belonged. The evil presence began to mock and laugh at me by saying that I didn't have any authority to cast him into the pit of hell. He began to choke my heart in such a powerful way that I felt that my life was fading away at that moment. I became very desperate for my life and realized that none of the spiritual warfare trainings that I received were working against Satan when I directly encountered him in my room.

Finally, I cried out to Jesus Christ with all my heart and strength, *"Jesus Christ, Please save me!"* Now the Holy Spirit was speaking to my spirit, *"James, Begin to praise the Lord, Jesus Christ and do not focus on Satan and his wicked evil power but fix your eyes on Him alone. Keep praising the Lord until you feel His presence begins to fill the room. When the light of God fills your spirit, soul, flesh and the room, then the darkness will flee. Only the light of God can swallow up the darkness of Satan."*

So I began to praise the Lord with all my heart, soul and might. As I was praising and singing unto the Lord, I was able to see that the evil figure (I felt that it was Satan himself) gradually became very agitated, but he was no longer able to attack me like he did prior to the moment that I started praising the Lord. While I kept on praising Him with all my strength for about 20 minutes ignoring Satan completely, then suddenly the evil figure left the room and the light came back on.

Then the presence of the Lord filled the room with His power, glory, and peace. I was able to feel God's peace and freedom from Satan's tight grip on my heart. I was able to breathe freely and my fear dissipated from my heart. I realized that the best spiritual warfare against the power of darkness was to call upon the name of the Lord and praising Him until

His presence filled my heart and mind and the room. Once His glory came into the room, Satan and his wicked evil creatures couldn't stand in His presence, glorious light and divine power. Then the Lord instructed me to study how the heroes of the Bible fought their spiritual warfare in the Old and New Testaments.

After thoroughly studying the Scriptures, the Holy Spirit directed me to develop a PowerPoint teaching on spiritual warfare entitled *"It is Written!"* It must totally focus on the mighty power of God in conducting spiritual warfare and not magnify or focus on the evil power of Satan. Once I created the teaching material, I was being led by the Lord to teach it to disciples throughout the U. S. as well as in the world.

Through this experience, I realized personally that I must absolutely focus on the mighty power of God to defeat any satanic attack of darkness. **The battle belongs to the Lord! As we rest in the mighty presence of God, His glorious light will swallow up the power of darkness and Satan's wicked evil schemes against us.** Wherever I have shared the *"It is Written"* teaching, which is one of my Global Harvest Network (GHN) equipping courses, multitudes of participants have been set free from engaging in misguided spiritual warfare against Satan in the U. S. as well as in the world.

As they are focusing on exalting the Lord and His mighty power in the midst of Satan's spiritual attacks, God begins to fight the battle for them. And they have been set free from becoming unnecessary casualties because of engaging in the unauthorized spiritual warfare against the devil. As I have interviewed intercessors that have been binding Satan, principalities and powers of darkness during their spiritual warfare prayer sessions, many of them admit that their homes, family members, businesses and churches have been severely attacked by Satan since they launched their attacks against him. Now let us closely study how the New Testament

Scriptures direct us to deal with Satan and his wicked powers of darkness so that we will know how to conduct our spiritual warfare correctly.

HOW CHRIST DEFEATED SATAN'S TEMPTATIONS

After Jesus Christ was filled with the Holy Spirit, He returned from the Jordan and was led by the Spirit into the wilderness to be tempted for forty days by the devil (Luke 4:1-2). While Jesus Christ was in the wilderness, He ate nothing and was hungry. And the devil said to Him, "*If You are the Son of God, command that these stones to become bread* (Matthew 4:3)." But Jesus answered him saying, "***It is written**, 'Man shall not live by bread alone, but by every word that proceeds from the mouth of God* (Matthew 4:4).'" Satan was tempting Jesus Christ to misuse His power to support His personal need. First of all, Jesus Christ will never do anything directed by the devil, and secondly, He will never demonstrate His power to meet the desires of His flesh.

Then the devil took Him up into the holy city, set Him on the pinnacle of the temple, and said to Him, "*If You are the Son of God, throw Yourself down. For it is written: 'He shall give His angels charge over you. In their hands they shall bear you up, lest you dash your foot against a stone* (Matthew 4:5-6).'" Jesus said to him, "***It is written** again, 'You shall not tempt the Lord your God* (Matthew 4:7).'" The devil was tempting not only Jesus Christ to demonstrate His faith in the Father God by throwing Himself from the pinnacle of the temple, but also tempting the Father to fulfill the Scripture by protecting Him as He fell. However, as Jesus Christ declared, "*You shall not tempt the Lord your God,*" He was also claiming Lordship over the devil and rebuked his evil intention against him. Again, the devil took Jesus Christ up on an exceedingly high mountain, and showed Him all the kingdoms of the world and their glory. And he said to Him, *"All these things I will give You* (or in Luke 4:6 *"for this has been delivered to me, and I give it to whomever I wish"*) *if You will fall down and worship me."* Then Jesus said to him, *"**Away with you, Satan**! For **it is written**, 'You shall worship the Lord your God, and Him only you shall serve* (Matthew 4:8-10).'"

According to the above Scriptures, after the fall of Adam and Eve, the kingdoms of the world had been delivered to the devil. Therefore, the last Adam, Jesus Christ came to take back the authority over the kingdoms of the world that the first Adam lost to the devil. The devil's desire was and is and always will be for the kingdoms of the world to worship him so he even dared to ask Jesus Christ, the Son of the living God to fall down and worship him. However, Jesus Christ rebuked him by saying *"**Away with you, Satan**!"* and commanded him to only worship the Lord his God. Then the devil left Him and angels came and ministered to Him.

During the course of Christ's first direct encounter with Satan, He never bound him nor did He cast him into the bottomless pit even though He had the power to do so. Jesus Christ knew very well that Father God had an appointed time to send an angel to bind Satan and cast him into the bottomless pit in Revelation 20:1-3 and to throw him into the lake of fire in Revelation 20:10. Until then, even Jesus Christ couldn't disobey the will of Father God and bind Satan before his appointed time. So He simply said to Satan, *"**It is written!**"* and quoted the Scriptures to rebuke him. He also said *"**Away with you, Satan!**" instead of binding him.* If that was what Jesus Christ did in the Scriptures, then how much more should we follow His example for dealing with Satan's attacks and temptations in our lives. If Satan comes to you when you are sick in bed and says, *"You will die!"* you must not listen to His lies and attempts to cause you to fear. You simply need to declare, *"Away with you, Satan! It is written! By the stripes of Jesus Christ, I was healed."* And you must not directly engage in binding Satan or begin to fight against him with unauthorized authority of using the name of Jesus Christ. If you do, then Satan has power to attack and torment you by releasing a spirit of fear to bind your mind and heart in his greater bondage. However, if you rebuke Satan in the same way Jesus Christ did, then he will have to flee from you because Jesus will arise within you to defeat him with His authority and power—Satan is no match to the resurrected Lord Jesus Christ.

EXAMPLES OF CASTING OUT DEMONS IN THE NEW TESTAMENT

Jesus Christ cast many demons out of a man in Luke 8:26-35:

> *Then they sailed to the country of the Gadarenes, which is opposite Galilee. And when He stepped out on the land, there met Him **a certain man from the city who had demons for a long time**...When he saw Jesus, he cried out, fell down before Him, and with a loud voice said, **"What have I to do with You, Jesus, Son of the Most High God? I beg You, do not torment me!"** For He had commanded the unclean **spirit to come out of the man.** For it had often seized him, and he was kept under guard, bound with chains and shackles; and he broke the bonds and was driven*

by the demon into the wilderness. Jesus asked him, saying, "What is your name?" And he said, "Legion," because many demons had entered him. And **they begged Him that He would not command them to go out into the abyss.** Now a herd of many swine was feeding there on the mountain.

So **they begged Him that He would permit them to enter them.** And He permitted them. Then **the demons went out of the man and entered the swine**, and the herd ran violently down the steep place into the lake and drowned... Then they went out to see what had happened, and came to Jesus, and found the man from whom the demons had departed, sitting at the feet of Jesus, clothed and in his right mind. And they were afraid.

As we examine the above encounter with a demon-possessed man, we can discover a few facts about how Jesus Christ dealt with many demons:

- When Jesus Christ commanded with authority the unclean spirit to come out of the man, **the demon recognized who He was** and called Him "Jesus, Son of the Most High God."
- The unclean spirit begged Jesus Christ not to torment him.
- There were many demons in him but I believe that it was the strongest one that answered Christ's question and identified their name as "Legion."
- **They begged Jesus Christ not to command them to go out into the abyss.** That means they recognized Him as God who had the power to cast them into the abyss.
- When they begged Jesus Christ to permit them to enter into a herd of many swine, He permitted them. We can clearly see that **Jesus had the absolute authority** over

the Legion of demons and they had to obey His command. However, Jesus didn't cast them into the abyss before their appointed time.

Therefore, when Jesus Christ gives us His authority to cast demons out of a man, we can also do as He did utilizing His name. Then, demons have to obey our command in His name. We can destroy the works of the devil in the name of Jesus Christ as He declared in 1 John 3:8b, *"For this purpose the Son of God was manifested, that He might destroy the works of the devil."*

Jesus Christ rebuked the unclean spirit and healed a child in Luke 9:37-42:

> *Now it happened on the next day, when they had come down from the mountain, that a great multitude met Him. Suddenly a man from the multitude cried out, saying, "Teacher, I implore You, look on my son, for he is my only child. And behold,* ***a spirit seizes him, and he suddenly cries out; it convulses him so that he foams at the mouth; and it departs from him with great difficulty, bruising him.***
> *So I implored Your disciples to cast it out, but they could not." Then Jesus answered and said, "O faithless and perverse generation, how long shall I be with you and bear with you? Bring your son here." And as he was still coming,* ***the demon threw him down and convulsed him.*** *Then* ***Jesus rebuked the unclean spirit, healed the child****, and gave him back to his father.*

We can identify a few facts about how Jesus Christ dealt with the demon possessed boy:

- We do not know exactly how old the boy was, but we can clearly see that the unclean spirit entered into the child and greatly tormented him. Then the spirit departed from him but only with great difficulty and by bruising him. That means we need to pray over our children and exercise the authority of Christ over the demons so that they will never possess or afflict them.
- The disciples of Christ could not cast the spirit out of the boy. Without having total faith in Christ, not everyone can cast demons out of a person in bondage.
- When Jesus Christ called the boy to be brought to Him, the demon didn't want to be cast out so he threw the boy down and caused him to convulse.
- Once again, Jesus Christ rebuked the unclean spirit with His authority and healed the child. Jesus also commanded His disciples to cast out demons in Matthew 10:8. If we have faith to believe that we are in Christ and He is in us (John 14:20), then we can exercise the delegated authority of Christ to cast any demons out of a person.

Lord, even the demons are subject to us in Your name in Luke 10:17-20:

Then the seventy returned with joy, saying, **"Lord, even the demons are subject to us in Your name."** *And He said to them, "I saw Satan fall like lightning from heaven. Behold,* **I give you the authority** *to trample on serpents and scorpions, and over all the power of the enemy, and* **nothing shall by any means hurt you.** *Nevertheless do not rejoice in this, that the spirits are subject to you, but rather rejoice because your names are written in heaven.*

When Jesus Christ gave His authority to cast out demons to the seventy common followers, they were able to cast out many of them in His name. In the name of Jesus Christ, we can also cast any demons out that are binding people. As so many people were set free from the bondage of demonic powers, Satan lost his power over the region and fell like lightning from the second heaven. The above event occurred before Jesus Christ died on the cross and was resurrected.

Likewise, it also took place before the day of Pentecost when the Holy Spirit came down upon His disciples. In those days, when the seventy followers came back to Christ, His authority and power in them would return to Him because they were living prior to the Cross and Resurrection of Jesus Christ. If Jesus Christ wanted to send them out again to destroy the works of the devil, then He had to release His authority and power back to them to be empowered to do His work in His name.

If it was God's will for Christ to release His kingdom authority and power to the seventy common followers before the Cross, then how much more is it His desire for us to move in His authority and power to destroy the works of the devil now. We live after the events of the cross, resurrection and day of Pentecost and Jesus Christ indwells in us with His authority and the Holy Spirit with His power. Therefore, if Jesus Christ wants to use us to cast out demons, His indwelling authority and the Holy Spirit's power can be released through us as we obey His commandments.

When the demon was cast out in Matthew 9:32-33 and 12:22-23:

> *As they went out, behold, **they brought to Him a man, mute and demon-possessed. And when the demon was cast out, the mute spoke**. And the multitudes*

> *marveled, saying, "It was never seen like this in Israel!"* (Matthew 9:32-33)

> *Then one was brought to **Him who was demon-possessed, blind and mute**; and He healed him, so that **the blind and mute man both spoke and saw**. And all the multitudes were amazed and said, "Could this be the Son of David?*" (Matthew 12:22-23)

According to the above events, the man's blindness and mute condition can be as attributed to the works of demons. As Jesus Christ cast out the demon, the blind and mute man both saw and spoke. Therefore, we, the disciples of Christ, must cast demons out of many people who are afflicted in the name of Jesus Christ so that they can be healed of various diseases, including blindness and muteness. However, not all sicknesses are inflicted by demons so we need God's wisdom to wisely discern when we are to engage in casting out demons.

When an unclean spirit goes out of a man in Matthew 12:43-45:

> *When an unclean spirit goes out of a man, **he goes through dry places**, seeking rest, and finds none. Then he says, '**I will return to my house from which I came**.' And when he comes, he finds it empty, swept, and put in order. **Then he goes and takes with him seven other spirits more wicked than himself**, and they enter and dwell there; and the last state of that man is worse than the first. So shall it also be with this wicked generation.*

The above teachings of Jesus Christ clearly prove that we can cast demons out of a person; however, they will not be thrown into the abyss immediately after they have been cast out. **They will roam through the dry places of the earth looking for other victims to possess.** Or they may go back to the same one. When the unclean spirit goes back to the one that he had possessed before and finds out that one's temple is empty, then he can bring seven other spirits more wicked than himself to possess him or her again. The consequence of that is described as *"the last state of that man is worse than the first."*

There is a very important lesson in this for us to learn. After we cast demons out of a person, we must lead that person to the Lord Jesus Christ to be a born-again believer. Then, we need to pray that he or she will be filled with the Holy Spirit. In this way, his or her temple will not be simply empty of demons but is filled with the divine fruit and gifts of the Holy Spirit and life of Christ.

Jesus rebuked the demon, and he came out of him in Matthew 17:14-18:

> *And when they had come to the multitude, a man came to Him, kneeling down to Him and saying,* **"Lord, have mercy on my son, for he is an epileptic and suffers severely; for he often falls into the fire and often into the water.** *So I brought him to Your disciples, but they could not cure him." Then Jesus answered and said, "O faithless and perverse generation, how long shall I be with you? How long shall I bear with you? Bring him here to Me." And* **Jesus rebuked the demon, and it came out of him; and the child was cured from that very hour.**

On this occasion, a man brought an epileptic son who had been bound by a demon to the disciples of Christ to cure him, but they couldn't. It was obvious that the boy's epileptic condition was the result of demonic possession. Jesus Christ rebuked them as a faithless and perverse generation. Then He cast the demon out of the boy and he was cured from that very hour. Once again, **Jesus exercised His authority to cure the boy by casting out the demon**. We, the sons and daughters of God, also need to exercise the authority of Christ in faith and cast out demons that are tormenting multitudes of people. Jesus Christ, who is in believers, wants to use them to destroy the works of the devil in people's life so they can have eternal life and divine health.

The Apostle Paul's encounter with a sorcerer in Acts 13:6-12:

*Now when they had gone through the island to Paphos, they found a certain sorcerer, a false prophet, a Jew whose name was Bar-Jesus, who was with the proconsul, Sergius Paulus, an intelligent man. This man called for Barnabas and Saul and sought to hear the word of God. But **Elymas the sorcerer (for so his name is translated) withstood them, seeking to turn the proconsul away from the faith.***

*Then Saul, who also is called Paul, filled with the Holy Spirit, looked intently at him and said, **"O full of all deceit and all fraud, you son of the devil, you enemy of all righteousness, will you not cease perverting the straight ways of the Lord?** And now, indeed, the hand of the Lord is upon you, **and you shall be blind, not seeing the sun for a time."** And immediately a dark mist fell on him, and he went* *around seeking someone to lead him by the hand. Then the proconsul believed, when he saw what had been done, being astonished at the teaching of the Lord.*

According to the above Scriptures, Paul was trying to share the word of God to the proconsul but the sorcerer sought to turn him away from the faith. Paul was filled with the Holy Spirit and rebuked the evil intention of the sorcerer. And he pronounced the judgment of God upon him that he would be blind for a time. On this occasion, Paul didn't cast the demons out of the sorcerer; rather, he caused the sorcerer to become blind so that the proconsul could believe in faith.

In February 1994, I was conducting an open-air meeting in Bangalore, India for over 5,000 people. When the time came for me to preach, two local witches came right in front of the platform and began to chant something I couldn't understand. As they chanted, I started to have difficulty focusing on preaching and their evil acts really began to annoy me. So I had to stop preaching and ask my interpreter what they were chanting about. My interpreter sheepishly stated that they had been cursing me with their chanting. Therefore, I asked the Holy Spirit what I should do about that. Immediately, the Lord commanded me to pronounce His judgment upon them to become mute in the name of Jesus Christ.

I commanded the two witches to become mute in His name until I finished preaching. Suddenly, they fell to the ground and became silent. After I finished my message, I ordered them to stand up and I cast demons out of them. When I had the altar call, they also surrendered their lives to the Lord Jesus Christ. I have learned that when evil witches were trying to hinder my message, I needed to take authority over them and cause them to be silenced so God's message could be proclaimed. That night, over a thousand people gave their lives to the Lord during the altar call and many received God's supernatural healings.

Satan and his demonic powers of darkness have only one intention against the disciples of Christ—to steal, and to kill, and to destroy whatever God has ordained them to do for His glory on earth. Therefore, we need to resist Satan by drawing ourselves closer to the light of Christ and cast demons (footsoldiers of the devil) out of demonized people.

THREE TYPES OF KEYS IN THE NEW TESTAMENT

A function of a key is to allow or permit entrance, or to lock or forbid the privilege of passage. So, each different key has its own unique function of permitting or forbidding entrance to someone. Only the right key can open a specific entrance to a designated location to fulfill its purpose. A wrong key cannot be used to bind someone and cast him into a place where the key doesn't fit into a lock to open that door. The New Testament talks about three different types of keys:

1. *THE KEYS OF THE KINGDOM OF HEAVEN*

Jesus Christ gave the keys of the Kingdom of Heaven to His church (each believer in Christ) according to Matthew 16:18-19:

> *Now I say to you that you are Peter (which means 'rock'), and upon this rock I will build my church, and all the powers of hell will not conquer it. And I will give you* ***the keys of the Kingdom of Heaven.***

> *Whatever you **forbid** on earth will be **forbidden** in heaven, and whatever you **permit** on earth will be **permitted** in heaven"* (NLT)

The above Scriptures have been misused and misinterpreted to suggest that Christians can bind Satan and his powers of darkness on earth because the NKJV of the Bible used the words in verse 19 as follows: *"Whatever you **bind** on earth will be **bound** in heaven, and whatever you **loose** on earth will be **loosed** in heaven."* In Hebrew culture, for binding is to **disallow or forbid**, and the Hebrew for loosing is to **allow or permit**. Therefore, the above New Living Translation (NLT) Bible translates Matthew 16:19 more correctly in accordance with the Hebrew culture. The same principle also applies to another frequently quoted Scriptures (Matthew 18:18) by spiritual warfare teachers to justify their teachings on "binding and loosing."

Now let us examine who are the keys of the Kingdom of Heaven? All believers in Christ are the keys of the Kingdom of Heaven. Jesus Christ was the Master key of the Kingdom of Heaven and He made all of His born-again believers to become duplicated keys of the Kingdom of Heaven. The key of the Kingdom of Heaven will only open or permit other believers to enter into God's Kingdom. Thus, if we use the key of the Kingdom of Heaven to bind Satan, then we have to send him back to heaven but he is never allowed to enter back into heaven ever again. **In order for believers to bind Satan and to cast him into the bottomless pit, they must have the right key—the key to the bottomless pit.** In reality, the key of the Kingdom of Heaven can only be used to lead someone to heaven.

When I was ministering in India one time, I encountered a demon-possessed man. He was very strong and had beaten up several deacons of the church where I was ministering. They came to me with bruised faces and asked me to go and deliver the demon-possessed man. I reluctantly went with them because it was only the third time I ever tried to cast demons out of a man. The other two cases were young ladies who were bound by demons and they were not so strong and violent like this man.

My heart was filled with fear as I came closer to the demon-possessed man's home. I acted as though I was very confident in Christ outwardly, but I was frightened and fearful inwardly. I prayed silently in the Spirit and was asking the Lord to protect me from this demon-possessed man. When we arrived in front of his door which was slightly open, seven deacons pushed me into the room where the demon-possessed man was sitting. When he saw me, he became very angry and began to charge toward me swinging his tightened fist toward my face. His eyes were bulging red and they were not the eyes of a human being but of demons.

He was hissing and cursing as he charged at me. I didn't know what to do, so I screamed in fear and said, *"Jesus, Save me!"* When I said that, he stopped in front of me with his fist still pointing at my face. But he was frozen in a stationary position and didn't move at all for a while. When I looked at his eyes, strangely they were filled with fear and he was trembling before me as though he saw something that made him fearful. I didn't know what was going on at that moment. So I commanded him to sit down in Jesus' name.

All of a sudden, he began to behave like a child and sat before me quietly. He relaxed his fist and gently laid his hand on his right thigh. The Holy Spirit began to give me some words of knowledge about his childhood, how his own father had abused him and how he had lost his mother when he was 7-years-old. When I began to tell him about his past hurts and he had never been loved by anyone, he began to weep. But I told him that God loved him so much that He sent His own

Son to pay the penalty of his sin on the cross in order to give him a new life. As I was trying to lead him to Christ, many demons began to manifest. I spent the next 45 minutes casting many demons out of him. Finally, he was set free and surrendered his life to Jesus Christ. After he was totally delivered from all demons, I asked him why he charged at me at first, but then stopped suddenly in front of me and became almost like a frozen statue with great fear in his eyes. He told me that he saw a man who was shining with a very bright light standing behind me. When he saw him, he became frozen with fear and wasn't able to move at all. Then I knew Jesus Christ was protecting me from the angry demons in his body. I praised the Lord with all my heart when I heard that from him. What a mighty God we serve!

I, as a key of the kingdom of heaven, was able to lead the man to God's kingdom because I knew he was permitted in heaven when he gave his life to the Lord Jesus Christ. Therefore, each and every born-again believer of Jesus Christ is a key of the kingdom of heaven. Believers are the only ones who know the Gospel of Jesus Christ and the only way to the kingdom of heaven.

THE MISSIONS OF THE KEYS OF THE KINGDOM OF HEAVEN

All of the born-again children of God (the keys of the kingdom of heaven) are called to do God's divine missions on the earth.

1) **Preach the Salvation Plan of God:** As a key of the kingdom of heaven, we must preach the Salvation Plan in Matthew 10:7, *"And as you go, preach, saying, 'The Kingdom of Heaven is at hand.'"* Jesus Christ came to this world as the Lamb of God who would take away the sin of the world (John

1:29). The wages of sin is death (not only in this world but also eternal death in hell), but the gift of God is eternal life in Christ Jesus our Lord (Romans 6:23). Only believers in Christ can open the door to the kingdom of heaven to the lost and dying souls in the world by preaching the Salvation Plan of God as the Scriptures described in Romans 10:13-15:

> *For "whoever calls on the name of the Lord shall be saved." How then shall they call on Him in whom they have not believed? And how shall they believe in Him of whom they have not heard? And how shall they hear without a preacher? And how shall they preach unless they are sent? As it is written: "How beautiful are the feet of those who preach the gospel of peace, who bring glad tidings of good things!"*

Therefore, one of the most important duties of every born-again key of the kingdom of heaven is to do all he or she can to preach the gospel of Jesus Christ to the lost and dying souls in our own Jerusalem and in Judea and in Samaria and to the end of the earth. Once we are in Jesus Christ, then God's divine protection will be with us all the days of our life if we faithfully remain in Him by obeying His commandments. Because Noah obeyed God's commands to cover the ark inside and outside with pitch (Genesis 6:14)—the ark was completely sealed, so it could float safely on top of the floodwaters.

Thus, everyone inside the ark that Noah built was safe and sound. The pitch kept the water out. The word "pitch" is the same word used in one place for "atonement" (Leviticus 17:11). Jesus Christ, our Atonement is the "pitch" that keeps the floodwaters out from our lives. You may be experiencing storms coming toward you, but if you are inside the ark of safety—the Lord Jesus Christ—by being born-again in Him, then you have been covered and sealed from within and without. The enemy cannot destroy you no matter how hard he tries as long as you stay in the ark—Jesus Christ.[14]

2) **Demonstrate the Kingdom Plan of God:** Jesus Christ came to die on the cross as the Lamb of God to take away the sin of the world, but He was resurrected from the grave as the Lion of Judah to sit on the throne of King David as the King of kings and the Lord of lords. Once anyone is born-again in Christ, He comes and dwells inside of him to release His kingdom authority to him (Matthew 28:18). When the Holy Spirit comes upon him, He will empower him to move in God's kingdom power to minister in signs, wonders, and miracles to set people who have been bound by the evil power of darkness free in Jesus' name (Acts 1:8).

> ***All authority*** *has been given to Me in heaven and on earth.* (Matthew 28:18)

> *But **you shall receive power** when the Holy Spirit has come upon you; and you shall be witnesses to Me in Jerusalem, and in all Judea and Samaria, and to the end of the earth.* (Acts 1:8)

Therefore, Jesus Christ restored God's kingdom authority and power back to God's born-again sons and daughters so they can move in His Kingdom Plan to destroy the works of the devil and expand His Kingdom to the end of the earth to every Unreached People Group in the world. God's divine missions for His sons and daughters are not only for them to preach the Salvation Plan of God, but also to demonstrate the Kingdom Plan of God according to Matthew 10:7-8:

And as you go, preach, saying, 'The kingdom of heaven is at hand.' **Heal the sick, cleanse the lepers, raise the dead, cast out demons.** *Freely you have received, freely give.*

As the sons and daughters of God demonstrate the Kingdom Plan of God in action, many unbelievers will see their signs, wonders, and miracles and believe that Jesus Christ is the Lord and Savior. Jesus Christ gives us power to live the life He called us to live. We can live victoriously through any attacks that we might face by the power of God dwelling within us. 1 John 4:4 states, *"Greater is He who is in you than he who is in the world."* Many Christians have hardly lived a minute of victory or peace since their salvation. They simply do not know that the same power that brought them out of their sin can keep them in victory as they trust the Lord and allow His power to manifest through them to destroy the works of the devil each day.[15]

I would like to share one of my stories of God's divine healing that caused a Buddhist lady and her whole family to become born-again believers in Christ in Myanmar. One day I was conducting a revival meeting at one of my disciple's church in Yangon. It was a newly planted church with around 30 attendees. After I preached a revival message at the church, I invited anyone who would like to give his or her life to the Lord Jesus Christ to come forward. During the altar call, seven people came forward to surrender their lives to the Lord. That was my preaching of the Salvation Plan.

After that, I asked anyone who needed physical healing to come forward to the altar and five people came forward to receive my prayer of healing. As I prayed for them one by one, the mighty power of the Holy Spirit began to fall upon each of them and they all fell by the power of God. They were all under the power of the Holy Spirit for almost 20 minutes and they began to get up one by one. All five of them declared that they were healed by the power of God that night. I was very excited about their supernatural healings. One lady told me that she was totally healed of her breast cancer because she couldn't feel the tumors in her breasts as well as there was no longer any pain in her body. But she told me that she was a Buddhist and she wanted to surrender to the Lord Jesus Christ because she felt the touch of God who healed her of cancer.

She said to me, *"I prayed to Buddha to heal me every day three to four hours for two years, but I became worse and the cancer spread to other parts of my body. However, when you prayed for me, I felt the power and heat come down upon me and I was sweating and shaking uncontrollably for 20 minutes. Finally, when I slowly got up, I was able to feel that I was totally healed. So I want to know who Jesus Christ is. I want to believe that He is the real God who answered my prayer."*

After she, a Buddhist lady, experienced a miracle healing for herself, it was very easy for me to lead her to the Lord Jesus Christ. Therefore, demonstrating the Kingdom Plan will glorify Jesus Christ and cause unbelievers to surrender their lives to Him.

3) **Destroy the works of the devil:** Initially, God gave the first Adam and his descendants the authority to rule over every living thing on the earth in Genesis 1:26:

> *Let Us make man in Our image, according to Our likeness;* ***let them have dominion over…all the earth*** *and over every creeping thing that creeps on the earth.*

Therefore, Jesus Christ, the last Adam, came to take away the dominion authority over all the earth from Satan that he usurped from the first Adam to become the ruler of this world. Under Satan's rule over the earth, he released all sorts of sins, sicknesses, curses and the fear of death to every living soul that ever lived on the earth. Nevertheless, Jesus declared in John 12:31, *"Now is the judgment of this world; now **the ruler of this world will be cast out**. And I, if I am lifted up from the earth, will draw all peoples to Myself."* Also Jesus said in John 14:30, *"I will no longer talk much with you, for **the ruler of this world is coming, and he has nothing in Me**."* Again Jesus said in John 16:11, *"of judgment, because **the ruler of this world is judged**."* In order for Jesus Christ to judge the rulership of Satan on the earth, He came to destroy the works of the devil until he will be cast into the eternal lake of fire in the future.

Thus, we read in 1 John 3:8b, *"For this purpose the Son of God was manifested, that **He might destroy the works of the devil**."* For Jesus Christ to destroy the works of the devil, He needs all born-again sons and daughters of God to manifest His presence in their lives wherever they go. So they can set people free from the works of the devil that have been revealed in sicknesses, unbelief, demonization, depression, oppression, addiction, curses, suffering, the fear of death, etc. While Jesus Christ was walking and ministering on earth before He went to the cross, His credentials were written in Matthew 11:5-6:

The blind see and the lame walk; the lepers are cleansed and the deaf hear; the dead are raised up and the poor have the gospel preached to them. And blessed is he who is not offended because of Me.

The normal Christian life is not just attending a church service on Sundays, enjoying social fellowships and home groups on weekdays. But it is all about each of His sons and daughters being the Church and allowing Jesus Christ to manifest Himself through him or her to destroy the works of the devil every day. Jesus Christ lives inside of us with all authority in heaven and on earth and the Holy Spirit lives inside of us with all power to control the whole universe. Therefore, we can destroy the works of the devil in the name of Jesus Christ as He gives us His delegated authority and power to do so.

That is why, Jesus Christ commanded us in Matthew 10:7-8, *"And as you go, preach, saying, 'The Kingdom of Heaven is at hand.' Heal the sick, cleanse the lepers, raise the dead, cast out demons. Freely you have received, freely give."* After the Day of Pentecost, Peter and John demonstrated Matthew 10:7-8 in Acts 3:1-8. One day, they received the authority from Jesus Christ to heal a certain man lame from his mother's womb who was placed daily at the gate of the temple which was called Beautiful. When Peter told him to look at him and he declared, *"Silver and gold I do not have, but **what I do have I give you**: In the name of Jesus Christ of Nazareth, rise up and walk."* The important question is ***"Do you know what do you have after becoming a believer in Jesus Christ?"***

Peter and John destroyed the works of the devil over the man who had been crippled his whole life. As a result of that miracle, their normal Christian lives began. You and I can do the same because Jesus Christ's authority and the full power of the Holy Spirit reside in us. We only need to receive **the power of attorney from Jesus Christ to execute His order** to destroy the works of the devil every day. We, too, can begin to live the normal Christian life with signs, wonders and miracles following.

As the keys of the kingdom of heaven, sons and daughters of God can also cast (not bind) demons (Satan's foot soldiers) out of the people who have been possessed by them **on the**

earth. We need to realize that even though the demons can be cast out of a person, afterwards they will be free to roam around the earth to bind another person as their victim. However, God didn't give us any authority to bind principalities, powers, the rulers of the darkness of this age, or spiritual hosts of wickedness **in the heavenly places** (in the second heavenly realm).

Then, how can we block the assaults of the evil forces in the heavenly places over our lives, businesses, cities, states, and nations? The best way for sons and daughters of God to do this is to pray and repent of their sins, and by asking God to bring His justice, righteousness and revival to the wicked leaders, situations and circumstances over the city, region, and nation. Then, He can dispatch His mighty warrior angels to fight against the spiritual hosts of wickedness in the heavenly places on behalf of His children's petitions just like He did for Daniel in Daniel 10:12-13 and 19-20.

The devil has no patience; therefore, it is vital to know that as we wait on the Lord to fight the battle for us, it is the devil that gets frustrated. He likes quick gains and easy targets to attack. We need to make it hard for him by growing in God's grace and in the fruit of the Holy Spirit. If we make it a point to move in the power and fruit of the Holy Spirit every moment of our life, then everything the devil throws at us will only make us stronger. In this way we make him frustrated and confused because we are not taking his baits to launch spiritual warfare directly at him. We demoralize the devil when we choose the Spirit of life.[16]

One of the most deadly and cunning tactics of the devil that has been launched against the Church is that of religious spirits. Let's examine more deeply the difference between Jesus' life-giving Spirit (Romans 8:1-2) and that of the Pharisees' religious spirits. The religious spirits have been in operation among fallen mankind ever since the fall of man.

The heart of the religious spirits demands that we work very hard to achieve God's favor, gifts, freedom, deliverance, healing, and abundant life on earth and eternal life in heaven. However, all the blessings that come down from God, including salvation, healing, deliverance, gifts and fruit of the Holy Spirit, abundant life on earth, divine health, provisions, blessings, anointing, baptism of the Holy Spirit, and the like, are all freely given to His children.

No one can receive them by works of religion led by religious spirits. They are free gifts for those who will surrender their lives to Christ in faith. Therefore, all those blessings of God can only be received by believing in faith in Jesus Christ—by repenting of our own sins, ways, works, depending on religious spirits and teachings, traditions, rituals, etc. Thus, the Bible declares in Ephesians 2:8, *"For by grace you have been saved through faith, and that not of yourselves; it is the gift of God, not of works, lest anyone should boast."*

The Pharisees, who were led by religious spirits, had an ethic of avoidance, whereas Jesus Christ, who led by the Spirit of life, had an ethic of involvement. The Pharisee's question was not *"How can I glorify God?"* It was *"How can I avoid bringing disgrace to God?"* This degenerated into a concern not with God, but with self—with image, reputation, procedure, tradition, ritual, and religious laws. They didn't ask, *"How can I make others clean?"* They asked, *"How can I keep myself from getting dirty?"* They did not seek to rescue sinners, only to avoid sinning by obeying the man-made laws and traditions led by religious spirits.

Jesus Christ, in sharp contrast, got involved. He sought always and in all ways to help, to heal, to save, and to restore. Rather than running from evil, He ran toward the good. And evil, in fear, fled. Look at the man who had been bound by the legion of demons. Everyone else feared the demon possessed man, tried to banish him to the tombs. But when Jesus Christ showed up, it's the legion of demons that were afraid, begging Him not to torment them and to command them to go out into the abyss (Luke 8:27-33). Jesus Christ has come to seek and save that which is lost, not to destroy. He cast the legion of demons out of him and restored him to community. Jesus Christ is not the least bit afraid of the legion of demons. Rather, the demons in Legion feared the holy power in Jesus Christ and are subdued by it. Darkness always flees when light shines.[17] In the same manner, the children of God must not be afraid of the devil and his wicked evil schemes of darkness, but only fear the Lord and do the work of the kingdom of God by shining the light of Christ to every wounded, hurting and dying soul.

2. *THE KEYS OF HADES AND DEATH*

Jesus Christ will be the judge of the living and the dead according to 1 Peter 4:5. Also 2 Timothy 4:1 states, *"who will judge the living and the dead at His appearing and His kingdom."* The final proof that Jesus Christ will be the judge of the living and the dead is because He has the keys of Hades and Death according to Revelation 1:18, *"I am He who lives, and was dead, and behold, 'I am alive forevermore, Amen. And I have the keys of Hades and of Death."*

That means Jesus Christ has the right keys to judge those who die without repenting of their sins and accepting Him as the Lamb of God who takes away the sin of the world. Therefore, Jesus Christ has the authority and power as well as the right keys to cast them into Hades and Death (commonly referred as Hell or Sheol where those who die without Christ would fall into). In reality, Jesus Christ relinquished the keys of the Kingdom of Heaven to the children of God so that they can lead as many souls as they can into the Kingdom with the right keys. Many spiritual warfare teachers even teach their followers to bind Satan and any evil powers of darkness, and then cast them into Hades or the Abyss (a bottomless pit) or Hell or the lake of fire. **Sons and daughters of God neither have the keys of Hades (Hell) and Death nor the key to the bottomless pit. Therefore, it is not authorized for them to use the keys of the Kingdom of Heaven to bind Satan and cast him into Hades or the bottomless pit because they do not have the right keys to do that.**

3. *THE KEY TO THE BOTTOMLESS PIT*

The Scriptures in "Revelation 20:1-3, 10" are the only time the Bible mentions binding Satan and describes God's appointed time for him to be bound and cast into the bottomless pit and the lake of fire:

> *Then I saw **an angel** coming down from heaven, **having the key to the bottomless pit and a great chain in his hand**. He laid hold of the dragon, that serpent of old, who is the Devil and Satan, and bound him for a thousand years; and **he cast him into the bottomless pit**, and shut him up, and set a seal on him, so that he should deceive the nations no more till the thousand years were finished. But after these things he must be released for a little while...The devil, who deceived them, was **cast into the lake of fire** and brimstone where the beast and the false prophet are. And **they will be tormented day and night forever and ever.***

As we examine the above Scriptures carefully, we see that God will send an (nameless) angel who has the key to the bottomless pit and a great chain in his hand to bind the dragon, that serpent of old, who is the Devil and Satan. The angel has the right key to bind Satan and cast him into the bottomless pit, but sons and daughters of God do not have the key to the bottomless pit but the keys to the kingdom of heaven. That is why Christians can never bind Satan with the wrong key. God never gave us the authority to bind Satan because it will be an angel's job in His perfectly appointed time.

Until that time, no angels, people of God or even Jesus Christ can bind Satan and cast him into the bottomless pit and eventually to the lake of fire. This is because over 7,000 Unreached People Groups (UPGs) in the world are yet to hear the Gospel of Jesus Christ. If Satan was bound before God's appointed time, then all UPGs would have to be cast into the lake of fire without ever hearing the gospel of Jesus Christ. The closure of the Great Commission in Matthew 24:14 must be fulfilled before Jesus Christ can come back and for Satan to be bound and cast into the bottomless pit:

*And this gospel of the kingdom will be preached in all the world as a witness to all the **nations** [in Greek "**ethne**": every people group], and then the end will come.*

When every people, tongue, tribe, and nation hears the Gospel of Jesus Christ, then the end will come and He will come back to be the Lord of lords and the King of kings to reign on the earth with the sons and daughters of God. Then the prophecy of Revelation 7:9-10 will be fulfilled in the near future:

*After these things I looked, and behold, a great multitude which no one could number, **of all nations, tribes, peoples, and tongues,** standing before the*

throne and before the Lamb*, clothed with white robes, with palm branches in their hands, and crying out with a loud voice, saying, "**Salvation belongs to our God who sits on the throne, and to the Lamb**!*

THE TRUTH ABOUT BINDING THE STRONG MAN

Jesus Christ healed a demon-possessed, blind and mute man, so that the blind and mute man both saw and spoke in Matthew 12:22-29. And all the multitudes were amazed and said, *"Could this be the Son of David?"* However, when the Pharisees heard it and said, *"This fellow does not cast out demons except by Beelzebub, the ruler of the demons."* But Jesus knew their thoughts, and said to them: *"Every kingdom divided against itself is brought to desolation, and every city or house divided against itself will not stand."* Jesus Christ went on to say, *"If Satan casts out Satan, he is divided against himself. How then will his kingdom stand?* He was continuously reasoning with them by saying, *"And if I cast out demons by Beelzebub, by whom do your sons cast them out? Therefore they shall be your judges. **But if I cast out demons by the Spirit of God, surely the kingdom of God has come upon you.**"*

So it is very clear that **Jesus Christ was talking about casting out demons (not about casting out or binding Satan)** by the Spirit of God so that the kingdom of God would be manifested upon the person who would be set free from many demonic spirits. Based on the above statements, Jesus went on to declare in Matthew 12:29, *"Or how can one enter a strong man's house (talking about the body of demon-possessed man) and plunder his goods, unless he first binds*

the strong man (*in this context:* ***the strongest demon inside the demon-possessed man***)*? And then he will plunder his house* (*the body of the demon-possessed man*)*."* So many spiritual warfare teachers are misusing the above Scriptures by interpreting the strong man as Satan. And they justify, based on their wrong interpretation of the above Scriptures, their practice of binding Satan as the strong man which is authorized by Jesus Christ in verse 29 above.

However, the above Scriptures must be interpreted correctly according to the original context Jesus Christ described. In the beginning of Matthew 12:22, Jesus had already cast out all of the demons that possessed the blind and mute man. So the whole context of the Matthew 12:22-29 deals with the issues raised by the Pharisees accusing Jesus Christ of casting demons out of the man by the power of Beelzebub, the ruler of the demons. Now Jesus Christ was explaining to the Pharisees that if Satan cast out Satan, then his kingdom couldn't stand because he would be divided against himself.

Then Jesus Christ went on to say that if he cast out **demons by the Spirit of God, surely the kingdom of God would come upon the man** who had been set free from demons. **That was Christ's main point in those Scriptures that He cast out demons by the Spirit of God.** Jesus Christ didn't mention casting out Satan at all but only talked about casting out demons in the above Scriptures. **Therefore, the right conclusion about the strong man in the above Scriptures is that it is not talking about Satan but about the strongest demon inside the demon-possessed man.**

One time I was casting demons out of a Russian man in a Baptist church that was located on the outskirts of Moscow in 1991. It was in my early days of missions' work in the nations and I was learning to cast out demons by being plunged into the situation where I had to cast demons out of a person. It took more than seven hours to cast all the demons out of Victor, the Russian man. During the process of casting the demons out of him, I would ask him if there were still more demons remaining inside of him. Then Victor would say, *"Yes, there are many more of them still inside of me."* I wasn't sure then if it was Victor who was speaking to me or the demons'. Anyway, I kept asking Victor if there were still more demons inside of him throughout the process of casting them out.

Eventually, I became very tired and weary of casting demons out of Victor because it went on for hours. However, at the very end, Victor told me that there was still the strongest demon called the spirit of Pharisee remaining inside of him. So I called the spirit of Pharisee to come out of him in the name of Jesus Christ. Finally, the strongest demon (the strong man described by Jesus Christ in Matthew 12:29) caused Victor to be greatly tormented in the process of coming out. When the spirit of Pharisee came out of Victor, he became totally freed from all the influence of demons in his life and he sat next to me like a calm little child.

As soon as Victor was delivered from all kinds of demonic spirits, I led him to accept Jesus Christ as his Lord and Savior. After Victor surrendered his life to the Lord, he was smiling and said to me in tears, *"Thank you very much for helping me to be freed from many demons inside of me. I was in demonic bondage since I was around 15 years old when I began taking drugs, drinking Vodka, having sex, smoking cigarettes, and being involved in witchcraft and many other evil activities. But I know now I am totally free in Christ."* In this account of casting many demons out of Victor, I also had to deal with the strong man inside of him—the strongest demon called a spirit of Pharisee in order to completely set him free.

FOR PULLING DOWN STRONGHOLDS

Many spiritual warfare teachers also utilize 2 Corinthians 10:3-6 out of context to teach that believers in Christ can bind Satan. However, we must carefully examine these verses to understand the correct meaning and interpretation for followers of Christ. Teachers of the Bible must not misguide the sons and daughters of God regarding engaging in unauthorized spiritual warfare that focuses more on the power of Satan than on magnifying God and His mighty power. So let's examine 2 Corinthians 10:3-6 carefully:

- Verse 3, *"For though we **walk*** [in Greek *"peripateo"*: conduct ourselves] *in the flesh, we do not **war*** [in Greek *"strateuo"*: soldier in active service] *according to the **flesh*** [in Greek *"sarx"*: **worldly mindset or belief system**]. *"*: Therefore, we can correctly translate verse 3 as *"For though we conduct ourselves in the worldly mindset, but as soldiers in active service for the Lord, we do not engage in a battle according to our worldly mindset or belief system."* The New Living Translation (NLT) version translates this, *"We are human, but we don't wage war as humans do."*

- Verse 4, *"For the **weapons*** [in Greek *"hoplon"*: tools, instruments, or armor] *of our warfare are not **carnal*** [in Greek *"sarkikos"*: pertaining to the fleshly or worldly mindset] *but **mighty in God*** [in Greek *"theos"*: God-fearing] *for pulling down strongholds* [in Greek *"ochuroma"*: fortress], *"*: We can correctly interpret verse 4 as, *"For the tools or instruments of our warfare are not based on a worldly mindset but with the fear of the Lord, we totally depend on God's mighty power to pull down* fortresses of religious, philosophical and human reasoning mindsets."* Pulling down strongholds (fortresses) in this Scripture is not talking about binding Satan at all. The NLT version states, *"We use God's mighty weapons, not worldly weapons, to knock down the strongholds of human reasoning and to destroy false arguments."* The main emphasis of the Scripture is that **the weapons of our warfare are mighty in God or we use God's mighty weapons.**

- Verse 5, *"**casting down arguments** and every high thing that exalts itself against the knowledge of God, **bringing every thought into captivity** to the obedience of Christ,"* The NLT version states, *"We destroy every proud obstacle that keeps people from knowing God. **We capture their rebellious thoughts** and teach them to obey Christ."*: Now it is obvious that this verse is totally talking about casting down arguments and every high thing that exalts itself against the knowledge of God, and it has nothing to do with fighting against or binding Satan directly in this context. The main point of the Apostle Paul's teaching in these Scriptures can be summarized as *"Paul's war was against the opposition to the truth of the gospel of Jesus Christ. His ultimate goal was to bring **every thought into captivity to the obedience of the truth of Christ.**"*

Therefore, no teachers of the word of God should teach believers to wage spiritual warfare directly against Satan by using the above Scriptures out of their original meaning and context. When I try to minister to Hindus, Buddhists and Muslims, I have to depend on God's mighty wisdom and power to cast down their religious and human reasoning in order for them to be opened to the message of the gospel of Jesus Christ. If I fail to bring their belief system, that have been deeply influenced by their religious mindset of strongholds, into obedience to the truth of Christ, then their spiritual eyes will not be opened to accept the true gospel of the Kingdom of God.

BE STRONG IN THE LORD AND IN THE POWER OF HIS MIGHT

The Scriptures in Ephesians 6:10-20 have been some of the most misused verses in the Bible to launch spiritual warfare against Satan and all of his wicked evil forces of darkness in the heavenly realm. In so doing many naive sons and daughters of God, who launched unauthorized spiritual warfare against Satan, have become needless casualties of his fury.

Let us carefully examine what the Apostle Paul was actually writing in his spiritual letter to his disciples in the church of Ephesus. If we consider Ephesians 6:10-20 as one of Paul's letters to Ephesian believers, then we can examine it with the following three parts in the letter: 1) the opening statement which is the most important point; 2) the main body of the letter to support his opening statement; 3) the concluding part to emphasize his main exhortation to his disciples in the church in Ephesus.

1) **The opening statement**: Paul wrote in Ephesians 6:10, *"Finally, my brethren,* **be strong in the Lord and in the power** *of His might."* He was encouraging the Ephesian believers to focus on the Lord and in His mighty power when they face many challenges from the power of darkness. Paul wasn't suggesting that they should focus on Satan and his wicked evil powers by launching direct spiritual warfare against them because they were lurking around to devour them with their

wicked schemes. His true meaning of the letter was not directing them to constantly study every move of Satan and his demonic powers in order to be prepared to launch spiritual warfare against them. I believe Satan wants the children of God to be more focused on his evil power and schemes than spending quality time with God. Only being in God's divine presence, sons and daughters of God can find His mighty power of protection written in Psalm 91. As we come closer to God in prayer, we will be strong in the Lord and in the power of His might.

2) **The main body of the letter** in Ephesians 6:11-17:

Put on the whole armor of God, *that you may be able* ***to stand against*** *the wiles of the devil. For we do not wrestle* ***against*** *flesh and blood, but* ***against*** *principalities,* ***against*** *powers,* ***against*** *the rulers of the darkness of this age,* ***against*** *spiritual hosts of wickedness in the heavenly places. Therefore* ***take up the whole armor of God***, *that you may be able to* ***withstand*** *in the evil day, and having done all, to* ***stand. Stand*** *therefore, having girded your waist with truth, having put on the breastplate of righteousness, and having shod your feet with the preparation of the gospel of peace; above all, taking the shield of faith with which you will be able to* **quench** *all the fiery darts of the wicked one. And take the helmet of salvation, and the sword of the Spirit, which is the word of God;*

* ***against*** [in Greek "*pros*"]: a better translation of "*pros*" would be **in regard to; about; according to; or, in relation to.**

Because of the English translation of *"pros"* as "against," the whole passage became very confrontational in nature in Ephesians 6:12. This translation has led many teachers of spiritual warfare to instruct their followers to fight against **Satan, principalities, powers, the rulers of the darkness of this age and spiritual hosts of wickedness in the heavenly places.** This, then, leads to binding them out of your life, business, church, city, region, and country in the name of Jesus Christ. As we have already discussed, believers have no authority to bind Satan and to do so will only lead to further attacks from him.

In Ephesians 6:11, Paul instructs his disciples to **take up the whole armor of God** that they might be able to stand **in relation to (instead of using "against")** the wiles of the devil. In this verse, Paul's main point is for the disciples to be aware of the wiles of the devil so they can stand firm with the full armor of God to be prepared for the potential assault of the devil. We can further correctly explain verse 12 by utilizing a better translation of *pros* as *"in relation to"* in lieu of *"against"*:

> *For we do not wrestle* **in relation to** *flesh and blood, but* **in relation to** *principalities,* **in relation to** *powers,* **in relation to** *the rulers of the darkness of this age,* **in relation to** *spiritual hosts of wickedness in the heavenly places.*

When we change the translation of *"pros"* to *"in relation to,"* we can better understand Paul's intention. Paul simply wanted the disciples in Ephesus to be aware of principalities, powers, the rulers of the darkness of this age, and spiritual hosts of wickedness in the heavenly places. The above evil forces dwell in the second heavenly realms and we are not authorized to launch spiritual warfare against them.

Because they all have the appointed time on earth authorized by the Father God, they will not be bound by your command even though you use the name of Jesus Christ. They will eventually be bound by an angel of God in Revelation 20:1-3 and will ultimately be cast into the lake of fire in Revelation 20:10.

Therefore, Paul was not, in any way suggesting that the disciples of Christ to go after Satan and his wicked forces in the heavenly places by binding them in the name of Jesus Christ. He was simply warning them to be aware of the devil's schemes in the heavenly realms. Therefore, Paul went on to recommend that they take up the whole armor of God so that they might be able to **withstand** (in Greek *"anthistemi"*: **resist**) Satan in the evil day.

Again, he wasn't suggesting that they fight against Satan, rather, he was exhorting them to put on the whole armor of God to **resist** Satan and his wicked forces. He further encouraged them to **stand** [in Greek *"histemi"*: **come to a halt**; fixed stand; established] which meant for them to come to a halt and stand in a fixed position while taking up the whole armor of God to defend themselves from the devil's wicked schemes. Those charging words of the Apostle Paul were primarily for standing in their defensive positions in relation to Satan's wicked schemes.

Once again, Paul charged the disciples of the church in Ephesus to **stand** *"having girded your waist with truth, having put on the breastplate of righteousness, and having shod your feet with the preparation of the gospel of peace; above all,* **taking the shield of faith** *with which you will be able to quench all the fiery darts of the wicked one. And take the helmet of salvation, and the sword of the Spirit, which is the word of God."* The emphasis of the above charges is to maintain a defensive posture. There is no evidence Paul is suggesting any offensive tactic against Satan.

3) **The conclusion of the letter** in verses 18-20: It is very important for us to understand that the conclusion reveals the true heart of the author:

> *"**Praying always** with all prayer and supplication in the Spirit, being watchful to this end with all perseverance and **supplication for all the saints**—and for me, that utterance may be given to me, that I may open my mouth boldly to make known the mystery of the gospel, for which I am an ambassador in chains; that in it **I may speak boldly**, as I ought to speak."*

If Paul were truly suggesting that the disciples in Ephesus directly engage in binding Satan and his wicked powers in the heavenly realms, then his conclusion would strongly exhort the disciples to employ spiritual warfare tactics against the devil. However, from the above verses we can clearly see that Paul was instructing his disciples to **pray always for all the saints** and not focus on fighting against Satan. Finally, Paul revealed his true desire for writing the letter as follows, *"I may open my mouth boldly to make known the mystery of the gospel."*

Therefore, Paul was charging the disciples to be aware of the devil's schemes by being strong in the Lord and in the power of His might. He was instructing them to put on the full armor of God so that they could withstand and resist the assaults of the devil and his wicked powers in the heavenly realms by standing firm in their positions in Christ. Ultimately, he was charging them to **pray** always for all the saints so **they could boldly make known the mystery of the gospel to those who never heard the Good News.** So Paul declares in 1 Corinthians 2:4, *"And my speech and my preaching were not with persuasive words of human wisdom, but in demonstration of the Spirit and of power."*

THE THORN IN THE FLESH

When I encountered any one of the spiritual warfare teachers in the past, they always utilized Ephesians 6:10-20 as one of their doctrinal bases for instructing Christians to bind Satan. However, if Paul was truly promoting the concept of binding Satan in the name of Jesus Christ, then it would be logical that he would do so himself when attacked by Satan. But when we examine 2 Corinthians 12:7-9, **a thorn in the fresh was given to Paul by a messenger of Satan, yet he did not engage in binding Satan.** Let's examine how the Apostle Paul dealt with his thorn in the flesh:

> *And lest I should be exalted above measure by the abundance of the revelations, **a thorn in the flesh was given to me, a messenger of Satan to buffet me**, lest I be exalted above measure. **Concerning this thing I pleaded with the Lord three times that it might depart from me**. And He said to me, "My grace is sufficient for you, for My strength is made perfect in weakness." Therefore most gladly **I will rather boast in my infirmities, that the power of Christ may rest upon me.***"

Here we see that rather than binding Satan, Paul solely pleaded with the Lord three times that the thorn in his flesh might depart from him. **If Paul was instructing believers to bind Satan in Ephesians 6:10-20, then he should be the one binding Satan in 2 Corinthians 12:7-9.** When Paul pleaded with the Lord three times to take it away from him, the Lord assured him that His grace was sufficient and that His strength would be made perfect in his weakness.

Therefore, based on how Paul responded to his own problem of being buffeted by a messenger of Satan, it is obvious that his instructions in Ephesians 6:10-20 were never intended to teach believers to bind Satan. We cannot take Scriptures out of context and use them as we want to teach our own doctrine of spiritual warfare. To do so would misguide multitudes of believers and plunge them into unauthorized battles against Satan that could cause serious consequences for them.

THE LORD REBUKE YOU (SATAN)!

There are warnings in the Bible against doing unauthorized spiritual warfare that can bring severe consequences. For example, in Jude 6, 8-10:

> *And I remind you of the angels who did not stay **within the limits of authority God gave them** but left the place where they belonged. God has kept them securely chained in prisons of darkness, waiting for the great day of judgment...In the same way, these people—**who claim authority from their dreams**—live immoral lives, defy authority, and scoff at supernatural beings. But even **Michael, one of the mightiest of the angels**, did not dare accuse the devil of blasphemy, but simply said, "**The Lord rebuke you!**" (This took place when Michael was arguing with the devil about Moses' body.) But **these people scoff at things they do not understand**. Like unthinking animals, **they do whatever their instincts tell them**, and so **they bring about their own destruction**. (NLT)*

According to the above Scriptures, the angels who did not stay **within the limits of authority God gave them,** have been kept securely chained in prisons of darkness, waiting for the great Day of Judgment. Therefore, not only angels but also humans must stay within the limits of authority God has granted for them. In the same way, Jude wrote that, these people—who claim authority from their dreams—live immoral lives, defy authority and speak lightly of supernatural beings (including Satan and fallen angels). Obviously, even during the days of Jude, there might have been so called "spiritual warfare teachers" who defied God's authority and spoke lightly of supernatural beings by binding Satan and fallen angels.

Jude went on to say that even Michael, one of the mightiest of the angels, did not dare accuse the devil of blasphemy, but simply said, *"The Lord rebuke you!"* Michael and Lucifer were archangels in heaven with equal power and authority prior to the fall of Satan. Therefore, if there was any angel who could bind Satan, it would have been the archangel Michael. However, Michael also knew that he could not do anything against Satan before the Father God's appointed time.

If Michael would bind Satan before his appointed time, then he would be acting outside of the limits of authority God gave him. Even though Satan was a fallen archangel, Michael still had respect for how God allowed Satan to be the ruler of this world and he dared not bring an accusation against the devil, but simply said, *"The Lord rebuke you!"* **If one of the most powerful archangels, Michael, wouldn't directly bind Satan, then a mere born-again human being shouldn't either**. Satan's future fate is under the absolute control and authority of Father God. Therefore, Jude went on to say that these people (spiritual warfare people who acted outside of God's given authority) scoff at things they do not understand.

Like unthinking animals, they do whatever their instincts (misinterpretation of the Scriptures) tell them and, as a result, **they brought about their own destruction.** These Scriptures should be a frightening warning to those spiritual warfare teachers who have been mocking and binding Satan and his evil powers of darkness in order to pump themselves up and promote their own selfish gains by selling their books, CDs and DVDs. However, when they launch their spiritual attacks directly against the devil by binding him and casting him into the bottomless pit, Satan, who knows the Scriptures, will have the legal right to come and tear them apart with his evil power.

As I have traveled to many nations to minister the message of the kingdom of heaven, I have frequently encountered many leaders of spiritual warfare in churches. Many of them were women intercessors in indigenous churches. They normally spend many hours a week praying and binding Satan and principalities over their regions. However, strangely enough, they rarely go out to their own cities to evangelize lost souls, heal the sick, or cast demons out of souls that had been possessed by them.

All they do in the church is to gather as many people as they can to conduct spiritual warfare against Satan and the evil forces of darkness in the heavenly realms. Whenever I encounter them, I always ask them about how their family members are doing. To my big surprise, almost all of them declare that as they began to lead the spiritual warfare intercessory prayer teams at their churches, Satan began to attack their husbands, wives, family members, sons and daughters in such a powerful way that they were under great distress. Their husbands or wives or their children were severely attacked by Satan with drug, alcoholic, sexual, gambling, or many other demonic addictions. If they were such powerful intercessors, then they should be able to protect their own family members from the attacks of Satan. Just like Jude 10 described, these spiritual intercessors brought about their own destruction by doing unauthorized spiritual warfare against the devil. **These people scoff at things they do not understand and they do whatever their instincts tell them** let by the teachings of many so-called spiritual warfare teachers. Be Aware!

A SIMILAR WARNING FROM THE APOSTLE PETER

The Apostle Peter also warns that those who despise the authority of God and presumptuously speak evil of supernatural beings (including Satan and fallen angels) will be destroyed or severely attacked by them. Their destruction is their reward of the harm they have done in 2 Peter 2:10-13:

> *He (the Lord) is especially hard on those who follow their own twisted sexual desire, and **who despise authority**. These people are **proud and arrogant**, daring even to scoff at supernatural beings without so much as trembling. But **the angels, who are far greater in power and strength, do not dare to bring from the Lord a charge of blasphemy against those supernatural beings**.*
>
> *These false teachers are like unthinking animals, creatures of instinct, born to be caught and destroyed. **They scoff at things they do not understand, and like animals, they will be destroyed. Their destruction is their reward for the harm they have done.** They love to indulge in evil pleasures in broad daylight. They are a disgrace and a stain among you. They delight in*

deception even as they eat with you in your fellowship meals. (NLT)

The Apostle Peter writes almost the identical message as the book of Jude. When two books of the Bible describe the same teachings, we need to heed their warnings and listen very carefully to obey what the Holy Spirit is speaking to us—sons and daughters of God. Let's examine the above Scriptures carefully together:

- ***He (the Lord) is especially hard on** those who follow their own twisted sexual desire, and **who despise authority**:* One of the grave sins spiritual warfare teachers commit is to despise God's ordained authority. If God, in His infinite wisdom, sets up an appointed time for Satan and all his wicked fallen angels to be punished and thrown into the bottomless pit and the lake of fire, then sons and daughters of God must respect God's authority and His timetable.

- *These people are **proud and arrogant**, daring even to scoff at **supernatural beings** without so much as trembling:* Unfortunately, when an intercessor rises up and binds Satan in front of the congregation, he or she can become very proud and demonstrate his or her spiritual arrogance by bringing attention to himself or herself. The Scripture describes very clearly that Satan and his evil powers of darkness are still supernatural beings and that intercessors must not scoff at them without having any fear.

    As I have explained, there is not a single Scripture in the Bible that instructs Christians to attack Satan and his evil forces of darkness and bind them in the name of Jesus Christ. However, many spiritual warfare teachers continue to misuse those Scriptures, that I wrote about in this book, out of their original contexts to lead intercessors to their own destruction.

- *But the angels, who are far greater in power and strength, do not dare to bring from the Lord a charge of blasphemy against those supernatural beings*: Why, then, is it that the angels in heaven, who have never committed any sins, do not dare to bring from the Lord a charge of blasphemy against those fallen angels? It is because the angels have absolute respect for the Lord and for what He has decided in His own wisdom and power to do with Satan in His appointed time. If the angels, who have more than enough power to bind Satan and all of his hosts of evil powers, would actually bind them before God's appointed time, then God's divine purpose as revealed in the Bible from Genesis 1:1 to Revelation 22:21 would have to be altered.

- *These false teachers are like unthinking animals, creatures of instinct, born to be caught and destroyed. They scoff at things they do not understand, and like animals, they will be destroyed. Their destruction is their reward for the harm they have done*: What a terrifying statement of God against those false teachers who have been teaching against the will and authority of God by binding Satan before his appointed time.

  The above Scriptures call the false spiritual warfare teachers unthinking animals and creatures of instinct who have been born to be caught and destroyed by supernatural beings (Satan and his evil forces in heavenly realms). Finally the Bible states, *"Their destruction is their reward for the harm they have done."*

At this point, **if you have been involved in carrying out wrongful spiritual warfare without knowing the consequences revealed in the Scriptures, then I pray that you will repent and ask the Lord to forgive you for being presumptuously engaged in it.** God is merciful and He will not only forgive you but also empower you to correctly conduct spiritual warfare by focusing on His mighty power and presence.

MY HELP COMES FROM THE LORD

In order for us to totally focus on God's mighty power and glory and have victory over every wicked scheme of the devil, then we must put our absolute trust in the Lord. We need to declare that our help comes from the Lord according to Psalm 121:1-8:

I will lift up my eyes to the hills—from whence comes my help? ***My help comes from the Lord****, who made heaven and earth. He will not allow your foot to be moved;* ***He who keeps you will not slumber****. Behold, He who keeps Israel shall neither slumber nor sleep.* ***The Lord is your keeper; the Lord is your shade*** *at your right hand. The sun shall not strike you by day, nor the moon by night.* ***The Lord shall preserve you from all evil;*** *He shall preserve your soul.* ***The Lord shall preserve your going out and your coming in from this time forth, and even forevermore.***

When we put our total trust in the Lord, He will preserve us from all evil and protect us in our going out and coming in all the days of our lives. The devil tries to entice us to be fearful of his wicked schemes so that we will directly attack him with our own will power. The devil knows the Scriptures so his intentions are always to cause us to disobey and take up our spiritual battle against him directly so he will have the legal right to attack us ruthlessly. We must not fall into the devil's trap, but rather put our trust in the Lord by saying, "My help comes from the Lord!"

- **My help comes from the Lord** who made heaven and earth: When we declare that, we know that mighty God will protect us and preserve us from every wicked scheme of the devil.

- **He who keeps you** will neither slumber nor sleep: if the Lord keeps us, who can be against us! The Lord who neither slumbers nor sleeps will watch over you day and night. His angels will cover you with their wings.

- **The Lord is your Keeper**: As you surrender all of your life, possessions, jobs, and ministries to the Lord, then He will keep you and preserve all things that belong to Him. He will cause you to dwell in His secret place and allow you to find rest under the shadow of the Almighty. In order for Satan to attack any of your possessions, jobs, and businesses that belong to God, then he has to go against Him and he will not prevail.

- **The Lord shall preserve you from all evil**: As you declare that "the Lord is my refuge and my fortress; My God, in Him I will trust," then He will deliver you from the snare of the fowler and from the perilous pestilence. Because you have made the Lord, who is your refuge, even the Most High, your dwelling place, no evil shall

befall you, nor shall any plague come near your dwelling (Psalm 91:2-3, 9-10).

- **The Lord shall preserve your going out and your coming in:** As you absolutely trust the Lord and magnify Him in your spiritual warfare, then He will give His angels charge over you to keep you in all your ways so that your going out and coming in will be preserved by the Lord forevermore.

CORRECT SPIRITUAL WARFARE AGAINST SATAN

Sons and daughters of God must conduct spiritual warfare correctly by respecting the authority of God according to the examples we have seen in Scripture. When they do so, then Satan and his wicked evil forces of darkness will be defeated as you magnify and focus on the Lord and His mighty power:

1) **Go and sin no more**: If we do our very best to live our lives free of sin, then Satan will have no power or legal right to attack us. Sin in our lives will always open a door for Satan to come against us with his wicked evil power. For instance, if we do not forgive sins of others, we will be tormented by the devil according to the words of Christ in Matthew 18:32-35.

Also, Isaiah 59:1-2 states, *"Behold, the Lord's hand is not shortened, that it cannot save; nor His ear heavy, that it cannot hear. But your iniquities have separated you from your God; and your sins have hidden His face from you, so that He will not hear."* Therefore, our sins will separate us from our God and He will not hear our prayers. So we also should consider ourselves to be dead to the power of sin and alive to God through Christ Jesus (NLT: Romans 6:11), then Satan will not have any part in us and we can live holy and pure life before God.

2) **Reflect the light of Christ** by praising Him in all circumstances—then Satan and his evil forces of darkness cannot stand in His light. Even in the midst of Satan's assault, we must not focus on his wicked schemes and be fearful, but, rather, we must fix our eyes on Christ and praise Him until His presence fills our hearts and minds. Then the power and threat of darkness will be dissipated by the light, presence and glory of Christ.

When I have encountered the evil forces of darkness on the mission field; firstly, I come to a place of being still before the Lord; secondly, I choose to totally ignore the devil and his evil threats against me; thirdly, I began to praise the Lord and acknowledge that His mighty power is all around me. As I do this, the light of Jesus Christ and His mighty presence defeats the devil. I never bind the devil, but I pronounce with the authority of Christ, **"the Lord rebuke you, Satan!"** Then, the evil force of darkness dissipates before me and God's presence and glory fills the place and my heart. Satan is no match to the resurrected Lord Jesus Christ who resides in us as we magnify Him and allow His light to shine out of us before the presence of the evil one.

3) **Submit (yield to a superior authority) to God and resist (succeed in ignoring the attraction of) the devil** until he will flee from you: When the devil tempts or assaults us as we begin to listen to him or to fight directly with him by binding him, then we are focusing on his evil power and his demonic attraction. The best strategy

against the devil is to ignore the attraction of his wicked schemes and resist his temptations. After then, we can begin to exalt the name of the Lord, Jesus Christ by praising His mighty power and His beauty of holiness until His presence manifests out of us according to His promise in John 14:21. Then the devil will flee before us because he cannot stand before the presence of the resurrected Christ.

4) **Draw near to God** in prayer and He will draw near to us: If God's hedge of Psalm 91 protection is around us, then Satan has no power over us. As we draw near to God, the devil will move away from us not because we resist him but because we draw ourselves near to God. When we are in the center of God's will and under His divine presence and light, Satan's darkness cannot come near us, because His light will swallow up any darkness around us. Then, we can declare Psalm 27:1 as our motto, *"**The Lord is my light and my salvation; whom shall I fear?** The Lord is the strength of my life; of whom shall I be afraid."*

5) **Magnify the Lord** until His glory and presence will manifest, then Satan cannot come near where God's glory dwells. The Scripture in 2 Thessalonians 2:8 describes, *"And then the lawless one will be revealed, whom the Lord will consume with **the breath of His mouth and destroy with the brightness of His coming.**"* As the brightness of His coming will destroy the lawless one in the near future, Christ's mighty presence around and upon us will expel every wicked scheme of the devil. As we bless and magnify the Lord in the midst of our spiritual warfare as the Psalmist did in Psalm 21:13, *"Be exalted, O Lord, Your own strength! We will sing and praise Your power."*; then He will fight the spiritual battle for us.

6) **Rebuke Satan by saying:** *"It is written!"* and quote the related Word of God to drive out the temptation of the devil. Just like Jesus Christ rebuked Satan with the Word of God and quoted the pertinent Scripture to defeat his evil intention or temptation, we can do the same. For example, when we become sick and the devil whispers in our ears that we will not be healed, then we can say to him, *"It is written! By the stripes of Christ I was already healed. Amen"*

   We can also say, *"**The Lord rebuke you**"* or *"**Get behind of me, Satan**"* or *"**You have no part in me.**"* Whatever Jesus Christ or the angels declared in the Bible against Satan, we can say as well to rebuke and resist him. Once we rebuke Satan according to the above-authorized ways, then we need to quickly ignore him and begin to magnify the Lord's mighty power over the situation and claim His victory at the cross over him. Then he will flee from us.

7) **Let the love, joy, and peace of God flow out of us** toward all people and situations: Satan cannot dwell with a person who chooses not to condemn, judge, criticize, hate, and have unforgiveness toward others. Satan can only indwell a person whose heart is filled with unforgiveness, bitterness, hatred, anger, condemnation, judgment, all kinds of additions, sexual immorality, prejudice, fear, doubt, worries, anxiety, and the like. We must let the love of Christ shine through our lives so the accuser of the brethren cannot have any part in us.

   As we meditate on whatever things are true, noble, just, pure, lovely and of good report, Satan will not have any part in us and the light of God will expel all darkness out of our hearts and minds through Christ Jesus.

THE DEAD WERE JUDGED

Ultimately, the devil, who deceived the whole world will be cast into the lake of fire and brimstone where the beast and the false prophet are. And they will be tormented day and night forever and ever. Furthermore, the Great White Throne of Judgment will be established and all the dead, small and great, will be judged according to their works on the earth in Revelation 20:11-15:

> Then I saw **a great white throne and Him who sat on it**, *from whose face the earth and the heaven fled away. And there was found no place for them. And I saw* **the dead, small and great, standing before God***, and books were opened. And another book was opened, which is* **the Book of Life***. And* **the dead were judged according to their works***, by the things which were written in the books. The sea gave up the dead who were in it, and* **Death and Hades delivered up the dead** *who were in them. And they were judged, each one according to his works. Then Death and Hades were cast into the lake of fire. This is the second death. And* **anyone not found written in the Book of Life was cast into the lake of fire***.*

According to the above Scriptures, Jesus Christ who has the keys of Hades and Death will judge the dead according to their works that were written in the books. Ultimately, anyone whose name is not written in the Book of Life will be cast into the lake of fire. Only Jesus Christ can judge the dead and cast them into the lake of fire because he has the right keys. Therefore, no one can bind Satan and cast him into the lake of fire because he or she doesn't have the right key.

Therefore, the sons and daughters of God must not waste their time conducting spiritual warfare against Satan in an incorrect manner. Rather, they must totally rely on God's mighty power to preach the Gospel of Jesus Christ to over 7,000 UPGs in the world. **Wherever we may go in the world, we need to move in God's kingdom authority and power to destroy the works of the devil by healing the sick, cleansing the lepers, casting out demons, and raising the dead (Matthew 10:7-8) with signs, wonders and miracles following until the day of the Lord Jesus Christ.**

We need to fear the Lord and rescue as many souls as we can from the lake of fire by using the Keys of the Kingdom of Heaven. As God walks with us, He will protect us from all the evil schemes of the devil and no weapon formed against us shall prosper. We will, indeed, be more than conquerors in Jesus Christ as we stand firm in His love no matter what we face in life such as tribulation, or distress, or persecution, or famine, or nakedness, or peril, or sword (Romans 8:35). **Let us fix our eyes on Jesus Christ who won the total victory over Satan at the cross, then He will fight every battle against the power of darkness for us:**

*"**The battle belongs to the Lord!** (1 Samuel 17:47)"*

AUTHOR'S PRAYER

Oh Lord! I pray that You will bless all the people who will read this book and empower them to find new life in Jesus Christ. May You guide them to focus on the Lord and Your mighty power to conduct their spiritual warfare and not on Satan and his powers of darkness! As they magnify the Lord, Jesus Christ and praise Your name in all situations and circumstances, Your presence and glory will fill their lives and expel every evil scheme of the devil out of their lives. May You empower them with the Kingdom authority and power to destroy the works of the devil and preach the kingdom of heaven from their own Jerusalem to the end of the earth. Amen!

REFERENCES

---

[1] Opal L. Reddin (1989). *Power Encounter* (P. 175-177). Springfield, MO: Central Bible College Press.

[2] John Paul Jackson (1999). *Needless Casualties of War* (P. 33-35). Fort Worth, TX: Streams Publications.

[3] Burton Stokes & Lynn Lucas (1988). *No Longer A Victim* (P. 11-14). Shippensburg, PA: Destiny Image Publisher.

[4] Sue Curran (1998). *I Saw Satan Fall Like Lightning* (P. 52). Orlando, FL: Creation House.

[5] John Eckhardt (2008). *Prayers that rout demons* (P. 81). Lake Mary, FL: Charisma House.

[6] Stephen Hill (1997). *White Cane Religion* (P. 124). Shippensburg, PA: Destiny Image Publishers.

[7] Burton Stokes & Lynn Lucas (1988). *No Longer A Victim* (P. 14-15). Shippensburg, PA: Destiny Image Publishers.

[8] Stephen Hill (1997). *White Cane Religion* (P. 125). Shippensburg, PA: Destiny Image Publishers.

[9] Dave Hunt & T. A. McMahon (1985). *The Seduction of Christianity* (P. 83-85). Eugene, OR: Harvest House Publishers.

[10] Rick Godwin (1997). *Exposing Witchcraft in the Church* (P. 52). Orlando, FL: Creation House.

[11] Jim Cymbala (2001). *Fresh Power* (P. 123-124). Grand Rapids, MI: Zondervan Publishing House.

[12] Rick Godwin (1997). *Exposing Witchcraft in the Church* (P. 53). Orlando, FL: Creation House.

[13] Houdmann, S. Michael, *What is a burnt offering?* Retrieved from https://www.gotquestions.org/burnt-offering.html

[14] Kenneth Hagin, Jr. (1993). *Speak to Your Mountain* (P. 117-118). Tulsa, OK: Faith Library Publications.

[15] Dean Sherman (1990). *Spiritual Warfare for Every Christian* (P. 120). Seattle, WA: YWAM Publishing.

[16] Graham Cooke (1999). *A Divine Confrontation* (P. 77). Shippensburg, PA: Destiny Image Publishers.

[17] Mark Buchanan (2001). *Your God is Too Safe* (P. 109). Sisters, OR: Multnomah Publishers.

ABOUT THE AUTHOR AND HIS MINISTRY

Dr. James Lee is the Founder and President of River of Life Ministries, whose mission is to equip indigenous Christian leaders through establishing the River Missions Training Centers (RMTCs) and conducting the Global Harvest Network (GHN) Conferences to plant indigenous churches among the Unreached People Groups in the world. He is also the Founder and President of Door of Hope Foundation, which carries out God's divine mission to bring the hope of Jesus Christ to facilitate charitable works that will enhance the welfare of the neediest and most vulnerable children and people in the world.

In 1985, Dr. Lee received the call to become a full time minister while stationed in the Flying Squadron 2 of NATO AWACS base in Germany as a senior Captain in the U.S. Air Force. Since he resigned his commission from the Air Force in 1987, he received his Master of Arts in World Missions and a Doctor of Ministry degree in Global Evangelization from Regent University in Virginia Beach, Virginia. Since 1988, Dr. Lee has traveled to more than 100 countries spreading the Gospel of Jesus Christ to multitudes of unreached people groups. He has equipped indigenous disciples through establishing RMTCs and conducting GHN Conferences. His disciples have planted over 800 indigenous churches worldwide. Dr. Lee is an apostle to the nations, an equipper of disciples, and an anointed evangelist with signs, wonders and miracles following in his ministries.

OTHER BOOKS BY DR. JAMES LEE

When God Walks with an Ordinary Man—A book which will inspire all believers in Christ to trust Him with all their hearts by allowing Him to walk with them to achieve His plan and purpose in their lives for His glory. God can empower His ordinary sons and daughters with His divine authority and power to accomplish His extraordinary tasks on earth as His special agents. In this book, Dr. Lee shares his divine encounters with supernatural God during his many missions' trips in the world. As you read this book, God will increase your faith so you can also do His divine works with signs, wonders and miracles following.

The Kingdom of Heaven is at Hand—Every believer in Yeshua the Messiah must understand God's overall mission for fallen mankind. Once the disciples of Christ truly grasps God's heart for the Israelites and the Gentiles, they must walk with the authority of Yeshua and the power of the Holy Spirit, demonstrating His kingdom presence in this dark world.

God's core mission is to utilize the Israelites to bring His Salvation and Kingdom Plans to bless all the families of the earth through the Son of the living God, Yeshua. The invisible Kingdom of Heaven has touched down on the Day of Pentecost. When this Gospel of the Kingdom is preached throughout the world, witnessing to all the families of the earth, then the end will come...

CONTACT INFORMATION

If God has made this book a blessing to you and you wish to share a testimony, or if you wish to be on the River of Life Ministries' mailing list to become a partner and receive our monthly newsletter, write to:

River of Life Ministries
P. O. Box 6128
Virginia Beach, VA 23456-0128
Web: www.rlmva.org
E-mail: riveroflife@rlmva.org
Tel: 757-554-0053

If you wish to support orphans and needy children in the world, then write to:

Door of Hope Foundation
P. O. Box 6261
Virginia Beach, VA 23456-0261
Web: www.doorofhopefoundation.com
E-mail: dhf@doorofhopefoundation.com
Tel: 757-271-6755

CPSIA information can be obtained
at www.ICGtesting.com
Printed in the USA
FFHW010931160120
57856953-63108FF